PET CARE
On a Budget

PET CARE
On a Budget

How to Cut Costs Without Compromising Care

by Virginia Parker Guidry

Howell Book House
New York

Howell Book House
A Simon and Schuster Macmillan Company
1633 Broadway
New York, NY 10019

Macmillan Publishing books may be purchased for business or sales promotional use. For information please write: Special Markets Department, Macmillan Publishing USA, 1633 Broadway, New York, NY 10019.

Library of Congress Cataloging-in-Publication Data
Guidry, Virginia Parker.
Pet care on a budget: how to cut costs without compromising care / by Virginia
Parker Guidry.
        p. cm.
ISBN 0-87605-643-5
        1. Pets.   2. Pets—Costs.   3. Budgets, personal.   4. Saving and thrift.   I. Title.
SF413.G825   1997
636.088'7—dc21   97-27632
                                                            CIP

Manufactured in the United States of America

10 9 8 7 6 5 4 3 2 1

Book Design: designLab, Seattle
Cover Design: George Berrian

Acknowledgments

Thanks to many people—friends, relatives and strangers—who inspired me with their thrifty ideas. Special thanks to Kim Campbell Thornton, the skilled and prudent editor, and Wayne J. Guidry, a king of thrift.

Table of Contents

Introduction

*Can anybody remember
when times were not hard,
and money not scarce?*
—Ralph Waldo Emerson

I f you're like most people, hardly a day goes by that you don't think, even worry, about money. Do you have enough to pay the telephone bill, the car insurance premium, the grocer? What day is payday? When is your next raise? What about saving for retirement or paying off debts?

Money isn't necessarily good or bad, but it is essential to living in this world, which is why we spend so much time thinking about it. Some believe having it brings happiness. To be sure, money allows freedom and choices that might be unlikely otherwise. One of those choices is owning a pet.

Apparently, it's an ever-popular choice in the United States. The American Veterinary Medical Association estimates there are some 200 million pets in the United States. And there's good reason for that number. The relationship between people and pets, called the *human-animal bond,* is very special and very strong. Companion animals—dogs, cats, birds, small mammals—enrich our lives. They offer friendship, companionship and love to those who choose to bring an animal into their home and family. Pets make us laugh, ease our loneliness, assist us, help us feel better when we're sick, even rescue us. Companion animals are God's special creatures, and we are fortunate to enjoy the wags, purrs and chirps they share with us.

But there's one point pet owners often forget: Owning an animal costs money. There's food to buy, veterinary care, training, housing and supplies. Without money, it's difficult to be a good provider for a pet.

Today's economic climate—increased cost of living, corporate downsizing and debt—has brought financial difficulties to many American families and their pets, which leads some to feel they must relinquish a beloved pet to a shelter or place the animal with a friend. Otherwise, they suffer personal hardships or compromise the animal's care. And some owners, through lack of planning, adopt a pet and find out a few months after they bring it home how expensive pet care can be. Other owners neglect their pets' care due to a lack of money.

It is my belief that when funds get tight, neither giving up a pet nor compromising on its care is a good solution. Our pets deserve the best we can offer and our utmost commitment to caring for them. Some argue that people who can't afford a pet shouldn't have one, and perhaps there is some truth to that. But animals don't care how much money you have; that's what is so beautiful about them. A pet will befriend a retiree living on Social Security as easily as a CEO with a fat salary. And who ever said that only those with income above a certain level are eligible to own pets?

The truth is, most families faced with cutting costs don't start out that way. A spouse might lose a job, income might fall and so on. Or an animal lover finds a stray and chooses to care for the animal rather than leave it on

Pets for the Masses

The American Veterinary Medical Association estimates there are 200 million pets of all types in the United States, and most of them are not the pampered pets of the rich and famous. According to a survey by the American Pet Products Manufacturers Association, 33 percent of all dog owners, 37 percent of cat owners, 40 percent of bird owners, 23 percent of reptile owners and 25 percent of small animal owners have a household income of less than $25,000 a year.

the street, even though he or she can't afford another pet. Eventually, the family pet gets penciled into the budget along with consolidating debt.

If you are feeling a financial squeeze and think you must give up a pet, this book is for you. Remember, the real problem isn't necessarily the pet. It may be how you're handling your money. Even if you're not feeling the pinch right now, it's always a good idea to economize. Make sure you have a little something put away in case your pet needs special veterinary care down the road, or just to buy you both a special present.

My goal in *Pet Care on a Budget* is to help owners cut costs without compromising care. Without a doubt, it takes money to own a pet. But it is possible to do it, and do it well, with less money than you might think.

Virginia Parker Guidry

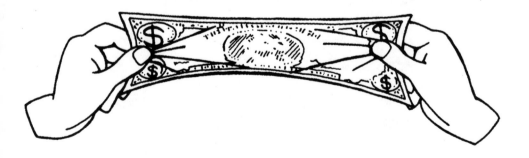

CHAPTER 1

The Five Points
That Make a Plan

When schemes are laid in advance, it is surprising how often the circumstances fit in with them.

—Sir William Osler

U.S. animal shelters are filled to the brim with beautiful animals whose only crime is that they belonged to an unprepared owner.

The story usually goes like this: An individual takes home a puppy, a kitten or a bird without giving it much thought. The animal is cute; it needs a home. End of story, or so the proud new owner thinks. The truth is, it doesn't end there. The tiny puppy grows into a big dog that digs up the yard, the kitten isn't healthy and runs up hundreds of dollars in veterinary bills or the bird is messy. The owner is frustrated, broke or both, and solves the problem—or so he or she thinks—by relinquishing the animal to a shelter. While the owner is rid of a frustration or financial burden, the pet's problems are just beginning. It may be placed in a good home, it may not. If not, it will probably be euthanized. At best, the future of a pet relinquished to a shelter is insecure.

The cycle of adopting a pet on impulse and getting rid of it when the owner is not prepared to meet its needs is a sad reality that need not happen at all. It can be prevented. All it takes is a little critical thinking—a plan. Following are five points to think over *before* you get a pet.

1

Point 1: Why a Pet?

No doubt about it, pets are irresistible, especially young animals. There's something about a small, fuzzy face and button eyes that can pierce a heart. It's fun to watch a kitten's antics and comforting to hold a cuddly bunny. Some owners describe meeting a special pet as "love at first sight" or "falling in love."

To be sure, the heart factor is an important part of owning pets. But that's exactly what gets owners into trouble: They act with their hearts and not their heads. They see a cute animal, take it home and a few months later realize they can't afford it, haven't a clue about housebreaking or didn't think the little thing would be so active.

Avoid this heartbreak altogether by asking yourself before you acquire an animal: *Why do I want a pet?* Be honest. Perhaps it's to help ease your loneliness or for protection. Or because they're beautiful or as a hobby to keep busy. Maybe you've seen similar animals and are simply fascinated by them. Those are good reasons, but they must be accompanied by a willingness to care for the animal through thick and thin. Pet ownership requires heartfelt commitment. A whim is never a good reason to get a pet.

Make sure your answer to why is a reason that will be true for years to come; that you are ready, willing and able to be a responsible and committed pet owner. Because that's what it takes to care for an animal properly. There's daily feeding, walking and cage cleaning, routine veterinary checkups, grooming, training and the associated expense—the list goes on and on. Owning a pet is much more than picking it out and taking it home. Many people don't know this until they've had the animal at home for a few months and are suddenly overwhelmed by the effort and expense.

Point 2: What Kind of Pet?

Amy Ammen, a Wisconsin dog trainer with 20 years experience, says it is essential for prospective owners to realistically evaluate the extent to which they can care for a dog. Ammen encourages buyers to think carefully about how much energy and effort they are willing to invest in the relationship. "A person must evaluate how lazy a dog owner he is. Many people are lazy dog owners and they end up with a Labrador Retriever and feelings of frustration because the dog is destructive."

Ammen's advice to puppy buyers applies to prospective owners of all species. What are you willing to invest, of your resources and of yourself? How much energy do you have? The answers to these questions will help determine what species, or what breed, will be appropriate for you. As Ammen notes, a lazy owner won't be happy with a pet that requires more effort than he or she is willing to give. Choose an animal that best suits your energy level—and be honest. For example, if you enjoy jogging, camping, hiking and other outdoor activities, a high-energy Labrador Retriever could be a good match. A sedate individual will be more comfortable with a cat or small mammal.

Lifestyle is another important factor in determining an appropriate pet. Are you home all day or do you rise early for work and return home after dark? Do you want an animal that will accompany you or one that can happily stay home? Pick an animal that best suits your lifestyle.

Which pets attract you? Some cherish cats, others like dogs or birds. Still others are interested in reptiles. Select a pet for which you have a natural affinity. Where you live can affect what kind of pet you choose, too. Pets have varying space requirements. Most large dogs need a backyard, although a large breed could live in an apartment with the right owner. Cats are suitable for apartments, condominiums or houses. Birds can be housed most anywhere, as can small mammals. If you do not own your house or apartment, don't forget to find out the landlord's pet policy. You may want a pet, but the owner of your home may say no.

Point 3: Estimate Costs

Whatever you do, don't omit this step. Failing to count the costs gets owners in big trouble. Don't buy on impulse, only to get trapped in money

What We're Buying

Shopping is America's favorite pastime. We love to wander about downtown merchant districts, stroll through malls, spend a work day lunch hour at a department store or, for animal enthusiasts, visit a pet supply store. And those visits prove profitable to pet supply retailers, who rake in billions from owners of all animal species.

Food is the animal enthusiast's most popular purchase, according to the *Pet Supplies and Marketing 1997 State of the Industry Report*, with dog food the tastiest item on the menu. After food, dog enthusiasts' favorite purchases are collars and leashes; owners spend some $54.3 million annually. Rawhide and other chew products followed close behind at $51.9 million in sales. Flea and tick products are the next most popular purchase.

Cats just wanna have fun and owners know it! Excluding food, toys are the cat enthusiast's primary purchase. Second to that are flea and tick products, then litter products.

Bird enthusiasts love purchasing feathered friends: Livestock sales totaled $232.9 million. Next are cages, toys and perches.

Not to be outpurchased, small mammal enthusiasts spent $70.9 million on pocket pets, $39.5 million on cages and enclosures and $31.3 million on treats and toys.

Last, but not least, reptile and amphibian enthusiasts spent $66.8 million on livestock, $17.6 million on heaters and nearly $15 million on accessories.

misery. Ask yourself: Do I have money to spend on a pet? Be realistic. If you're barely able to keep the lights on and are up to your ears in credit card debt, do not adopt a pet, no matter how cute it is.

That doesn't mean you need to own prime real estate to be a pet owner, but it may mean waiting. If you are itching for a pet but are currently broke, add a pet savings fund to your budget. Estimate how much money you need for the first year by calculating the pet's purchase price, food costs, basic supplies and veterinary care (Chapter 2 will help you figure out costs), and then save until you have enough. When you have extra cash after paying bills and adding to the pet fund, pick up supplies in advance, especially if they're on sale. There's nothing wrong with laying in a good stock of kitty litter before you bring the kitty home. Waiting is an unpopular notion to our I-want-it-now society. However, estimating care costs and waiting until you have enough money ensures you are committed to caring for an animal responsibly.

Point 4: Do Your Homework

A good potential owner has developed a well-thought-out plan. This includes going to the library, researching and reading. Perhaps this sounds more like school than acquiring a pet. It should.

Put some effort into learning about which animal species or breed is best for you. Don't be lazy about it; you'll reap what you sow. Read books and magazines, ask questions, join in animal forums on the Internet. For example, if you're interested in reptiles, read a reptile magazine, talk with someone who owns or breeds the species you're interested in and search the Internet for articles and information. Make sure you really understand what you're getting into, and that you know how to care for your pet. Do your homework *before* you get your pet.

Point 5: Shop Around

Okay, now the fun begins! You've thought about what kind of pet you want and why, and figured out how much it's going to cost. You've even done your homework. Now it's time to shop.

SHOPPING TIP

Shop seasonally. While it may require thinking and planning ahead, it can save money. For example, pick up Christmas stockings or toys for pets in January, or whenever retailers are discounting holiday items. Store them away for the next holiday.

Meet with breeders, and visit shelters, rescue groups and pet stores. Play with and handle the animal species in which you're interested. Is it really what you expect? Do you enjoy its company? For example, if you're looking for a Maine Coon kitten, talk with several breeders and make appointments to see litters. Find out if there's a rescue group in the area and check with the area shelter.

Don't be tempted to take home the first kitten you see. Avoid snap decisions. If you're really interested in a pet, ask if you can hold it (with a small deposit) for 24 hours so you can sleep on it. Reputable breeders are happy to comply, since they are in no hurry to send an animal to the wrong home.

Take your time and shop wisely. Remember, the animal you choose will be a family member for many years to come. Make sure you make a decision that leads to harmony in your home, not havoc.

CHAPTER 2
Count the Costs

> *Everything costs a lot of money when you don't have any.*
>
> —Joe Louis

The U.S. pet industry is a billion-dollar business. According to one report, Americans spend $20.3 billion a year on their pets, about half of that on veterinary care. Another report estimates $4.89 billion in sales at pet supply shops alone. Owners buy everything for their pets: food, toys, treats, bedding, housing, clothing, toiletries, even videos (bird-watching for cats!). They spend money on veterinary care, pet health insurance, training, competitions, birthday parties and burials. Pets fortunate enough to have a good home are better off than many children.

If you own a pet now, or have ever owned a pet, you can understand why the industry is booming. It's easy to spend money on an animal you adore. What does it really cost to own a pet and care for it properly, though? What expenses can you expect? Which expenses are mandatory and which are optional? Simply, what is the bottom line? To find out, let's consider some financial obligations you probably can't avoid:

- ✂ Adoption fee or purchase price

- ✂ Supplies

- ✂ Food

- ✂ Grooming

- ✂ Training

- ✂ Veterinary care

- ✂ Boarding

- ✂ Other costs

The potential for pet-care spending is incredible! Owners have never had so many animal-related products, foods or services from which to choose. But as wise consumers know, just because it's available doesn't mean it's necessary. For pet owners, it's important to draw the line between what's essential and what's optional. That's why for each of these categories I've included a little box that gives you some guidelines about what you can and can't do without. In addition, use common sense. If the product or service keeps the animal alive, safe and in good health, it's essential.

Adoption Fee or Purchase Price

SHOPPING TIP

If you're interested in a particular product on display in a pet supply store, ask to buy the floor model, which retailers will usually discount. Check the product carefully, though, for damage or dirt.

Even if you are adopting from a shelter, expect to pay something. The Humane Society of the United States estimates the average adoption fee for cats is $25; $55 for dogs. This may vary depending on animal species, state and shelter. If the organization doesn't ask for an adoption fee, consider donating anyway. Nonprofit organizations dedicated to helping animals always need financial help.

Buying an animal from a breeder or pet shop is more expensive, especially if the animal has a

pedigree. Expect to pay anywhere from $100 to $1,000 for a pedigreed cat or dog. Pure-bred rabbits are considerably less: $20 to $50. Ferrets, though not legal in every state, average $100 to $200. Rats, mice and guinea pigs average $10 to $15. Reptiles average $75, but prices vary widely, depending on the reptile. The purchase price of birds varies considerably: A budgerigar can cost a mere $10; a hand-fed cockatiel averages $60; medium-size parrots are $300 to $700; and large parrots (cockatoos, macaws) cost $700 to $8,000.

Additional expenses that add to your purchase cost include research (such as buying books or magazines), long distance telephone calls (not all breeders are in your area) and shipping.

Just the Essentials, Please!

Unless you have the extreme good fortune of inheriting a dream pet, an adoption fee or purchase price is a fact of life. What about animals that are advertised as "free to good home"? Don't count on finding one, but there are some wonderful pets available free to individuals willing to carry them home.

Supplies

This includes all those items essential (and sometimes not essential, but fun) to keeping a pet. Prices vary, depending upon where and what you buy.

Food and water dishes or bottles: Expect to spend $10 to $25 for dogs and cats, $5 for small mammals, $10 for reptiles. Collars and leashes: Nylon collars average $8, leather $15. Matching nylon leashes are about $8, leather $15 and up. Identification tags with the owner's name and address average $6 to $10. Chain training collars average $4. A nylon harness for a small animal can range from $6 to $8.

Cage, tank, crate, dog house or kennel: Small animal cages average $35. Figure on about $10 per 10 gallons for fish tanks. Bird cages are $75 and up. Crates range from $15 to $125, depending upon the size. Manufactured dog houses cost $50 and up.

Additionally, small mammals require bedding material, such as cedar chips, which average $15 a large bag. Reptile tanks need nonabrasive covering, about $5; heating, $10 to $30; and lighting, $15. And crates and dog houses need padding, $10 to $30. Toys can be as inexpensive as $1.98, but the average cost is $10.

Flea control products: Flea collars, $7; dip, $10; flea shampoo, $10; spray, $7; powder, $6; foam, $7; yard and kennel spray, $15.

Litter pan and scoop, $15. Litter is $4 to $5 for a 20-pound bag.

Just the Essentials, Please!

Before you buy, ask yourself if the animal can survive without it and, if you don't buy it, will the animal's care be compromised? Housing, for example, is essential. An animal cannot survive without it, at least not for long, and its care will be compromised. What about a toy? Well, it's unlikely withholding a toy will lead to a pet's demise. However, toys are not all fun and games. Toys entertain and alleviate boredom, and boredom leads to destructive behaviors in many animals. For instance, a toy is essential for a high-energy terrier that might otherwise eat the couch just for something to do. And birds with no toys can develop self-destructive behaviors such as feather-picking. Imagine yourself living all day, every day in a bare room with nothing to do.

Food

One of the biggest expenses of pet care, beside health costs, is food. It's not an option. Animals must eat daily (except for reptiles). The Humane Society of the United States estimates that a dog, depending upon its size, can eat anywhere from $115 to $400 out of an owner's budget each year. Cats cost less to feed at $145 a year. Birds average $240. The average-size rabbit eats a mere $30 to $40 in pellets a year; additional costs for fresh vegetables and greens are nominal. Ferrets eat $100 in food a year, and food for rats, mice and guinea pigs costs about $25 a year. Plan on $120 a year to feed a reptile.

Pet food prices vary depending on where, what and how much you buy. Costs are slightly higher at small pet specialty shops, lower at pet supply superstores and grocery stores. Additional dietary costs include treats, vitamins and supplements, or ingredients for homemade pet food.

Just the Essentials, Please!

Definitely essential! Food is not the place to economize, either: The better the food quality, the healthier your animal will be and the more you'll save on vet bills.

Grooming

Regular grooming, either by a professional or the pet's owner, is necessary for dogs, cats, rabbits (mostly those with long hair) and ferrets (to help minimize their pungent natural odor). If you opt for professional services, expect to pay handsomely for them. According to an American Boarding Kennels Association grooming price survey, cats average $20.88 per visit to the groomer. Dogs vary, depending upon the breed. The average price of a grooming session for a Miniature Poodle (haircut, bath, fluff dry, toenail trim, ear cleaning) is $22.98; for a Cocker Spaniel it's $26.82; a Schnauzer is $23.30; an Airedale is $31.77. Routine grooming (bath and brush) for a German Shepherd is $23.10; for a Collie it's $33.90; for an Old English Sheepdog (bath and brush out) it's $46.12. Expect additional charges for extra combing, at $17.95 an hour, and $5.86 for a flea dip. Toenail trims average $4.94.

Home grooming eliminates labor fees, but there is an initial investment to consider. Supplies might include:

- ✂ Professional animal clippers, $125 (blades are extra at $25 each)

- ✂ Professional scissors, $50

- ✂ Professional hair dryer, $125

- ✂ Grooming table, $80 to $100

- ✂ Nail trimmers, $8

- ✂ Styptic powder, $5

- ✂ Brush, $8

- ✂ Comb, $7

- ✂ Dematting tool, $10

- ✂ Shampoo (12 ounces), $8

Just the Essentials, Please!

Essential (unless you have a pet without fur), but the goal isn't a prize haircut, it's good health. This means you can pay for a professional groomer's services or do it yourself. If you do it yourself, the very least you'll need is a good brush and comb, scissors, nail clippers and a shampoo specifically formulated for your type of pet (human shampoos can dry the delicate skin of animals).

Training

While every animal needs some training and socialization, some obviously need a lot less than others. All an iguana needs is lots of time with you, to get accustomed to human contact and handling. A rabbit will also need socialization, plus some litter box training and possibly training to walk on a leash.

Dogs, because they are out and about with us every day, need perhaps the most training. Many people opt for classes, and they can be the best choice for your dog. Puppy socialization (also called puppy kindergarten) classes cost $50 to $120 for six to eight one-hour sessions. Beginning obedience classes are $50 to $90 for six to eight one-hour sessions. Private, in-home training with a trainer or animal behaviorist varies from $35 to $100 a visit, with no set number of visits. A trainer or behaviorist may also charge mileage or travel time.

Just the Essentials, Please!

Essential, and, as with grooming, you can pay for a professional trainer's services or train the animal yourself. If you go the second route, you'll at least need to buy a good training book or video.

Veterinary Care

The Humane Society of the United States estimates pet owners spend about $135 a year for their dog's medical care and $85 a year for their cat's. This doesn't include emergency services, long-term treatment for a chronic condition or consultation with a specialist, which can cost thousands.

According to a *Money* magazine survey of U.S. veterinarians, here are some typical veterinary costs:

	Dog	**Cat**
Office visit	$15 to $55	$15 to $55
House call surcharge	$15 to $25	$15 to $25
Basic vaccinations	$20 to $90	$20 to $110
Follow-up shots	$20 to $80	$20 to $78
Six-month heartworm preventive	$15 to $40	

	Dog	Cat
Declawing (front paws)		$25 to $145
Spaying	$35 to $145	$20 to $100
Neutering	$30 to $160	$15 to $60
Dental scaling	$35 to $200	$35 to $200
Chemotherapy	$300 to $3,000	$300 to $2,400
CAT scan	$300 to $700	$300 to $700
Magnetic resonance imaging	$250 to $1,000	$250 to $1,000
Euthanasia	$5 to $100	$5 to $75

While the majority of small animal practitioners treat cats and dogs, there is an increasing number of vets who see, or specialize in, health problems that afflict exotic animals: birds, reptiles, small mammals. Office visits and treatment costs vary, but expect to pay more for these specialists.

Just the Essentials, Please!

Good health care is definitely not optional. Visit a veterinarian regularly for vaccinations, annual exams or treatment when problems arise.

Boarding

Being away from home can mean additional costs for pet owners. According to an American Boarding Kennels Association survey of its members, the average charge to board a dog overnight is $10.53; the price may be slightly lower or higher according to the size of the dog. Boarding a cat is less at $6.80 a night.

A popular, but slightly more expensive, alternative to boarding is hiring a pet sitter. This also works for animals that would not do well in a boarding facility, such as birds and reptiles. The National Association of Pet Sitters reports an average price of $10.50 a visit; this price varies, depending upon the number and type of animals. Obviously, if the pet sitter makes more than one visit a day, the cost is even higher. However, many owners believe their pet is happier and less stressed by remaining at home during their absence.

Owners often ask a family member, friend or neighbor to care for their animals while away from home. In exchange, they'll pay a small fee or offer to do the same for their friend or neighbor. This is the exception, though, rather than the rule. And you must be sure the friend will visit every day and tend to all the tasks the care of your pet requires.

Just the Essentials, Please!

Whether or not boarding or pet sitting is essential really depends on you. If you're going to be away, it's definitely essential. The more frequently you travel, the more you must rely on someone else to care for your pets.

Other Costs

There are literally hundreds of things you can buy for your pet. Many are optional. Some, such as licenses, are not. Yearly licenses (if required) for dogs and cats average $15. Pet health insurance is available from several companies, with premiums costing anywhere from $50 to $225 a year. Pet magazines average $20 a year. Pet books are $10 to $50 each.

Professional pet burials start at about $100. Novelty items like coffee mugs, T-shirts, stationery and portraits vary in price—your self control is the only limit here.

Just the Essentials, Please!

While yearly pet licenses are mandatory in most states, items such as pet insurance or animal motif novelties are strictly optional.

If you've read this far, you can see how quickly pet care costs can add up, especially for veterinary care. Perhaps you've never considered the costs of owning a pet; you just know you'd like a pet of your very own. Don't be discouraged by the numbers. You can enjoy the companionship of an animal friend. Keep reading to learn how.

Minimum Annual Costs

Dog $1,200	Reptile $150
Bird $700	Rabbit $50
Cat $600	Small mammal $40
Ferret $300	

CHAPTER 3
Money
Management 101

*Dishonest money dwindles away,
but he who gathers money little by
little makes it grow.*
—Proverbs 13:11

Perhaps you are feeling discouraged after reading Chapter 2 and adding up the many costs associated with owning companion animals. This book is supposed to cut costs, not remind you of how expensive pet care can be. But as the saying goes, "You've got to begin at the beginning."

There's no better place to begin than by looking at how you're managing your money and attending to all aspects of your finances. This includes keeping records, saving for retirement or college, eliminating debt, buying a home, insurance, estate planning, lowering taxes and increasing income or investments. You can have the riches of King Solomon, but if you're not managing it properly you'll reduce it, waste it, even lose it—and you certainly won't be able to provide for a pet.

Like all skills, managing money is one that's learned. Infants are not born with an innate sense of the value of a dollar—though it is true that some individuals are naturally better at it than others (they grow up to be accountants). Anyone can learn how to look after their personal finances cautiously and responsibly, and everyone should!

The first lessons of money management are learned at home. Parents pass on their financial abilities, or inabilities, to their children. Children learn what they see around them. Chances are if your parents knew how to budget, save or keep out of debt, you do, too.

What's past is past, though. Eventually, children grow up, leave home and either take or reject the lessons they learned about money from their parents. Whatever you learned as a child can be embraced or cast off. In the case of managing money, if you lack skills you can develop them. If you're already skilled, you can always improve.

Let's take a look at what I believe to be the basic foundations of good money management. They're not based on some complex theory—just plain old common sense. If they seem simplistic, they're intended to be. Managing money properly so you can provide for a beloved pet doesn't have to be complicated. Perhaps that's what keeps many individuals from learning to be good stewards of their money. They think money management is difficult, complex, intimidating, a gift bestowed upon a few financial whizzes. To be sure, the world of finance is very complex. Without the guidance of an experienced financial planner, for example, a novice investor can find herself in deep trouble. However, the basic principles of managing your *personal* finances wisely aren't just for financial whizzes. They're for anyone who wishes to get fiscally fit.

What follows is an introduction, a beginning, to good money management. It's not intended to be a guide to your future riches, but a few suggestions on how to begin looking after your finances carefully so you can provide for a pet. Once you read over these ideas, you'll probably want to learn more. There are numerous, excellent books on the subject (written by financial whizzes) listed in Chapter 10.

Make an Effort

It's amazing how many people neglect their finances. But the truth is fiscal fitness doesn't just happen. Like physical fitness, it's the result of effort. Weight lifters, swimmers and aerobic enthusiasts don't work out once a month. They train several times a week, sometimes daily, to achieve good health and trim looks.

SHOPPING TIP

If you buy an item for your pet and take it home, will you be able to return it if necessary? Will you receive a cash refund or store exchange? A wise shopper takes note of a store's return policy. Find out before you buy to avoid disappointment.

If you're really serious about improving your financial health, realize that it requires effort. This is how that translates into real life: devoting 30 minutes or so a day to attending to your personal finances. That could be paying bills, balancing the checkbook, reviewing statements, planning a purchase—whatever needs attention. The idea is to make managing your money a daily or weekly habit. Doing so leaves no room for surprises at the end of the month, and it will keep your memory fresh as to what needs attention.

If you're afraid that devoting time and effort to finances means you're becoming a miser, don't be. (Unless, of course, you're stashing cash in a mattress instead of buying food for you and your pet.) You're simply performing financial exercises essential to good financial health. As Proverbs 27:23 warns, "Be sure you know the condition of your flocks, give careful attention to your herds."

Organize!

Get organized. You can't pay your bills if you can't find them amid the clutter on the kitchen table. Set up a designated home office area, complete with a file cabinet, folders, sorting baskets, paper, calculator, pens and the like. An organized workspace helps you take charge of your finances. For example, it means you can find receipts, statements or other important papers easily at tax time.

There's no right or wrong way of organizing—you don't have to use color-coded folders with typed labels. Do what works for you. However, here are a few suggestions. Use them as is, or adapt them to suit you.

- Managing your money is a business, according to Mary L. Sprouse, financial expert and author of *If Time Is Money, No Wonder I'm Not Rich*. As such, you need an office, or at least a desk in a quiet area of your home.

- Invest in a file cabinet and file folders.
- Purchase address labels or a rubber stamp with your name and address.
- Keep supplies, such as stamps and envelopes, on hand.
- Purchase "in" and "out" baskets.
- Use a monthly calendar. Mark deadlines, such as mortgage payments.

Keep Good Records

Keeping good financial records is important for several reasons. They tell you:

- What you own
- What you owe
- What you earn
- Where it goes

Armed with this information, you know exactly where you stand, no secrets, no surprises.

Don't toss financial records, such as bank statements and pay stubs. File them. Then take time each week to sort mail, pay bills and check the calendar for upcoming payments. Keep track of tax records, legal documents such as birth and marriage certificates, and insurance policies.

Don't leave documents lying around for curious pets to nibble (especially rabbits!) or children to mark with crayons. File them promptly and logically so you can retrieve them easily. Consider storing items such as a will or deed in a fireproof home safe or a bank safety deposit box.

Plan and Set Goals

If you're struggling to make ends meet, you may feel a touch of envy toward those who are enjoying financial freedom. It's natural to feel that way. But realize that a person's financial status isn't just the result of good or bad luck (though it is true some are just born into wealth). In most cases, financial success (which doesn't necessarily mean being rich, but does mean having a comfortable financial cushion) is the result of careful planning, responsible money management and an ability to set goals.

Regardless of how much, or how little, money you have in your bank account, if you haven't already, now is the time to establish your financial goals. A goal is simply another word for something you need or want: weekly groceries or new clothing. In order to achieve a goal, you need a plan. For example, your goal is to own a dog. At a minimum annual cost of $1,200, you must plan how you will pay for your pet. You might increase your income by working extra hours or redirect what you already earn. It's also good to set a timetable for reaching your goals. It helps motivate and gives you something to look forward to. Let's say it's June 1 and you wish to own a dog by the next January 1. That gives you six months to save money, buy supplies, research what breed you want, etc.

What are your financial goals, including pets? A great way to think this through is to get out a clean sheet of paper and a pencil and start writing (see financial goals worksheet on the next page). Make two lists: one for needs (food, housing, medical care, etc.) and one for wants (a parrot, a vacation in Europe). Following each goal, figure out what it will take to achieve it. This includes the dollar amount and specific action—a plan. Then estimate how long you need—a timetable. Some of your goals may be long-term, some short-term. Once you've listed each goal and its plan, prioritize the goals. What is really important to you? What can you really commit to? Be realistic: Dollars only go so far.

Another aspect of planning is determining what you spend, or budgeting. This is a very important aspect of good money management, but it's something that few people are willing to do today. Chapter 4 will take an in-depth look at budgeting, explaining why it's important to set up your own budget, and how to do it.

Avoid Debt

There are many pitfalls on the road to fiscal fitness, and the most dangerous one is debt. It's so easy to buy items today with money you don't have! Credit card companies, department stores, credit unions, car dealers and

Financial Goals Worksheet

Short-Term Goals	Need or Want?	Time Frame
1. _____	_____	_____
2. _____	_____	_____
3. _____	_____	_____

Plan for implementing Goal 1_____
_____
_____

Plan for implementing Goal 2_____
_____
_____

Plan for implementing Goal 3_____
_____
_____

Long-Term Goals	Need or Want?	Time Frame
1. _____	_____	_____
2. _____	_____	_____
3. _____	_____	_____

Plan for implementing Goal 1_____
_____
_____

Plan for implementing Goal 2_____
_____
_____

Plan for implementing Goal 3_____
_____
_____

a host of others too numerous to mention here are competing for your business. They are betting that your desire to have something *now* will win over your empty bank account. They are willing to extend credit—with the promise that you'll pay it back. The catch is you pay interest on the unpaid balance. That's extra money you could save or invest.

To be sure, some debt can't be avoided if you plan to buy very expensive items such as a house or car. Most people can't pay cash for a $200,000 home or a $20,000 car. Home and auto loans are reasonable debts. People more often get into trouble by taking on numerous small debts that add up to more debt than they can really afford. Money experts usually recommend that total debt, excluding your mortgage, should be no higher than 10 to 15 percent of your take-home pay.

Credit cards, which are so easy to obtain, are a main cause of this country's overindebtedness. Sure, you can charge a purchase today, but you must always remember that you will have to pay later. If you don't pay off the balance each month, figure on paying 18 to 21 percent interest, unless you're lucky enough to find a "low-interest" card at around 11 percent.

If you're already in over your head in debt, there's no better time than now to turn things around. And, realize now is not the time to think about adopting a pet. Seek out the help of a credit counselor (see Chapter 10 for resource information) or a money-savvy friend. Stop spending, charging and borrowing. Make a plan to eliminate debt and move forward. (For a thorough and helpful discussion on managing debt, see Chapter 6, "How to Manage Your Debt" in *The Money Book of Personal Finance* by Richard Eisenberg.)

Borrowing money wisely can enhance your life. But beware: It's easy to dig in deeper than you can manage.

Save

Saving is another essential aspect of good money management. It's so essential, it's covered twice in this book: here briefly and in depth in Chapter 5. The habit of setting money aside regularly, and letting your money earn money, is a good habit that will serve you well all your life. Saving for the future enables you to retire, pay for unexpected expenses, pay for your child's college tuition or take a once-in-a lifetime vacation.

There are many ways to save and invest, and these will be covered in Chapter 5. For now, if you're don't already have a savings plan, consider committing to one.

Research

Knowledge is power, right? That means if you understand the basics of managing money, you'll be in control of your finances. And that's a key issue. Many individuals let their money bus drive them, and end up careening down a mountain road into a ditch. Make an effort (there's that phrase again) to learn about finances. Drive your own money bus.

After reading this book, review Chapter 10 for suggestions on further reading. Go to the library and check out a few. Read personal finance magazines (available at the library), check out financial forums online. Learn how to estimate your net worth, prepare a budget, set up a savings plan.

Keep in mind that not everyone is cut out to be a professional financial planner. That's okay. Stick to the basics, and aim at learning enough to manage your personal finances wisely.

Get Help

There may come a time when you need help managing your finances. Knowing when and who to ask are the hallmarks of a wise money manager. In your search, you'll find numerous professionals who can advise and assist you on a variety of financial matters. But you must be careful to choose someone you can trust and afford, and who has the expertise you need. The best way to find an honest adviser of any type is to ask family members, friends and colleagues for names. A recommendation from someone you trust is the safest bet.

Following is a short list of financial-related professionals and the services they might offer. Be aware that how these titles are used can vary among financial experts, so make sure an individual or firm has the expertise you need. Find out how long the individual or firm has been in business, areas of specialty, credentials and fees. Check references carefully. Although you're seeking help, remember that *you* are ultimately responsible for how your money is managed.

✄ **Banker.** Need a checking or savings account, home or auto loan, safety deposit box or credit card? These are a few of the services banks offer. Shop carefully, because fees vary.

✄ **Tax preparer.** A skilled tax preparer can help keep money in your pocket, legally. According to Richard Eisenberg, author of *The Money Book of Personal Finance*, there are three types: storefront preparers, certified public accountants and enrolled agents. Storefront are the least expensive and most conservative. CPAs and enrolled agents are ideal for more complicated returns, as well as year-round tax planning advice.

✄ **Stockbroker.** For advice on investing in stocks and bonds, contact a reputable full-service stockbroker.

✄ **Insurance agent.** There are two types of agents: independent and agents who work exclusively for one insurer. Both can provide you with life, health, disability, homeowner's or auto insurance.

✄ **Financial planner.** These experts can provide you with a comprehensive financial plan, from setting goals to implementing a plan.

✄ **Money manager.** For those with plenty of money ($50,000 and up) to invest, this professional takes charge of all investments.

✄ **Lawyer.** If you need legal advice, especially concerning estate planning or taxes, contact a lawyer. Some lawyers specialize in tax law.

CHAPTER 4
Budget Time

Budgeting is the art of doing that well with one dollar which any bungler can do well with two.

—Arthur Wellington

Let's continue our look at basic money management with something that makes most people cringe. To some, it conjures up images of a scowl-faced tightwad counting out pennies and penciling in expenditures in a worn expense booklet. To others, it's a ball and chain. I'm talking about a budget, and in spite of all the negative associations, a budget is a pet owner's best friend.

A budget simply means planning for and assigning money to particular expenses. That's not so bad, is it? As author Rochelle LaMotte McDonald notes in *How to Pinch a Penny Till It Screams,* a budget is, in fact, extremely positive. It offers freedom from financial uncertainty and makes you the master of your money. When you don't follow a budget, although you may feel free at first, you actually become enslaved to debt and inhibit your financial growth.

Many times, financial difficulties are not due to living costs but are the result of poor money management. To be sure, pet-care expenses are real and should not be overlooked. However, managed properly, even a modest income can support a beloved pet.

There are many excellent resources—books, tapes, magazines—available with a variety of methods for and ideas about budgets. Generally, though, a budget identifies four items:

✄ Income (wages, salaries, investments)

✄ Expenses (what you actually spend)

✄ Goals (savings, eliminate debt)

✄ Progress (periodic reviews)

Figuring out this information need not be complicated, but it is important. Author McDonald compares a budget to a road map. Most people wouldn't dream of setting off on a long-distance road trip without a map; a budget is like a map for your financial future. A budget helps direct you to the right financial location. And if you're an animal lover, that location includes pets.

The first step in setting up a personal budget is to get a clear picture of where you stand by taking inventory of where your money goes each month and each year. You can't cut pet-care costs if you don't know how much you're spending!

Following is a sample budget worksheet. You can use this or make your own. Included are basic income and expense categories; expenses include fixed obligations (such as monthly rent or mortgage) and flexible obligations (vacation, recreation). Not all categories will apply, and you may want to add categories that are uniquely yours.

To use this worksheet, first calculate your income. (This is the amount of money you take home, not what you earn before taxes and other deductions are taken out.) Next, find out what you've spent by going through your checkbook, receipts and credit card bills for the past year. Where you don't have an exact figure, make the best guess you can. Place each expenditure in its proper category. While this exercise is time-consuming and somewhat tedious, it is important. Again, you can't cut costs if you don't know where your money is going.

Pet Owner's Personal Budget Worksheet

INCOME
Salary _____
Bonuses, tips (etc.) _____
Investments (interest, dividends, capital gains, real estate income) _____
Total Income _____

FIXED EXPENSES
Housing (rent or mortgage payments) _____
Utilities (gas, electric, water, telephone) _____
Taxes (federal, state and local, property, Social Security) _____
Interest payments (car, bank loan, credit cards, other loans) _____
Principle payments (amounts of borrowed principal repaid) _____
Insurance (health, life, property) _____
Education (tuition, room and board, supplies) _____
Contributions _____
Food _____
Transportation _____
Personal _____
Pets
    Food _____
    Grooming _____
    Veterinary care _____
    Other pet expenses _____

Total Fixed Expenses _____

FLEXIBLE EXPENSES
Clothing _____
Entertainment _____
Vacations, recreation _____
Furniture, appliances, home improvements _____
Health and beauty _____
Savings _____
Miscellaneous _____
Pets
    Toys _____
    Treats _____
    Other pet expenses _____

Total Flexible Expenses _____

Total Expenses _____

Amount available for investing, saving or adding to pet budget
(total income minus total expenses) _____

Once this task is complete, take a close look at how much you're spending and where. Does your spending match your income? Do you save money regularly or overspend with credit cards? Are there categories you can cut back or eliminate? What is really important? Study your money habits carefully, and then decide where you can cut back or where you might need to increase spending.

Now take the amount you spend per year in each category and divide it by 12 to arrive at a monthly budget. In other words, if you spend $1,800 a year on clothes, divide by 12 and that's $150 a month for your clothing budget. Add up all your spending for the month and you have your total monthly expenses.

Next, take the amount you earn in a year (after tax and any other deductions) and divide it by 12 to find your total monthly income. If you earn $22,000 a year, that's $1,833 a month.

Subtract your total monthly expenses from your total monthly income. If you end up with a negative number, you have some adjusting to do! Adjust the figures until the monthly expenses (including something put aside for savings) equal the monthly income. Now you have a budget.

Keep track of your monthly expenses. Tally spending for each category to see if it falls below or meets your budgeted expenses. Keep in mind that budgets are most helpful when you don't exceed the amounts specified in each category. Simply, don't rob Peter to pay Paul. If you have trouble sticking to a budget, review the budget to make sure it takes into account your actual expenses.

If budgeting seems overwhelming, consider cheating a little. Budget only what you spend on your pet, and review what you spend each month. You won't get a clear view of your entire financial status, but at least you'll have some idea of how much pet care is costing you.

Creating a budget means you're serious about managing money, which may include difficult choices. But if your goal is to have enough funds to provide for a beloved pet, tough choices sting only for an instant.

SHOPPING TIP

If you're prone to impulse buys, write out a list of exactly what you need before shopping. Remember to take the list into the store and mark off each item as you pick it up. Then head straight for the cash register.

Consider setting up a budget if you haven't already. That way, you can determine without a doubt if you can afford a pet. If you already own a pet, a budget can help you see where you might be able to redirect resources. Remember, it takes money to care for a pet properly. Do your best to manage your pennies carefully.

CHAPTER 5
Rainy Day Savings

Saving is a very fine thing.
Especially when your parents
have done it for you.
—Winston Churchill

Saving. It's a seemingly small word, but its meaning can move financial mountains, especially when it's teamed up with smart money management. Unfortunately, the art of saving money has been lost to the baby boom generation. Americans today are saving less than ever before, spending and incurring debt instead. What might be socked away for a rainy day or retirement is paid out in interest payments or applied toward the latest techno-gadget. After that, there's nothing to save.

If all this seems gloomy, it should. Spending money you don't have, using what you have foolishly, or both, is nothing to be proud of. Especially as children of Depression-era parents who were forced to save by sheer necessity, you'd think we knew better!

There is good news, too, and that's the focus of this chapter. You can break tradition with a spending generation, as many boomers are beginning to do, and save money. That may seem like a radical new idea, but it's really an age-old principle of smart money management. Consider Proverbs 21:20: "The wise man saves for the future."

Setting money aside regularly provides you with a cash reserve to meet any unexpected circumstances that could limit your earning power and drain your bank account. If you know you've got a reserve, you're less likely to become stressed when financial storms blow your way. For the pet owner, having a stash means you don't have to give up a pet or forego care when faced with a financial squeeze. Isn't that reason enough to save?

Remember reading about planning and setting financial goals in Chapter 3? That's another reason to save: to reach a goal. Perhaps you are renting an apartment now but have a dream of owning a home. That means a hefty down payment, which you probably don't have unless you've just won the lottery. A savings plan can make a dream like that come true, though it will require some sacrifices and waiting.

You can save for smaller goals, too, such as buying a purebred dog or a very special type of bird, or a very special piece of equipment for your pet.

Another plus for saving is preparing for retirement. If you plan for those years while you're young (financial experts recommend you begin saving for retirement as soon as you begin working), you're more likely to retire comfortably with little financial stress.

No matter how you look at it, tucking away money for the future makes good sense. It's true that you can neither predict nor plan everything that happens in life, but saving money helps prepare for the unexpected.

It's important for any individual to save, but especially important for those with dependents—human or animal. That means you, pet owners!

You're probably wondering if saving money is so sensible, why aren't more people doing? It's a good question that deserves answers. According to Ginita Wall, financial expert and author of *The Way to Save*, Americans growing up during the Great Depression in the 1930s acquired a respect for money as the result of witnessing financial disaster. Out of need, these folks became a generation of savers. But rising inflation after World War II changed all that. Money saved no longer had the same buying power. "As prices spiraled upward," writes Wall, "it was smart to borrow to purchase that new television or refrigerator, because the tax-deductible interest was less than the rate of inflation. *Our inflationary economic system rewarded spenders and penalized savers.*"

The result, says Wall, is a generation that mortgages the future to ensure the present. Borrowing and spending have become a way of life, an excepted norm, from individuals to businesses to government. "The United States became a debtor nation," writes Wall, "borrowing from its people . . . to keep the economy solvent."

In addition, we have become a nation of consumers. Shopping, buying and accumulating goods is a favorite American pastime. (Whether or not it brings happiness is questionable.) We are bombarded with slick advertisements on television, on billboards, in the mail, on the Internet and everywhere else we look, aimed at reinforcing and encouraging buy-shop-buy-shop behavior. If you don't believe it, just walk into a mall on Saturday or Sunday afternoon. It's *the* place to be. It's packed with kids, teens and adults, all wandering in and out of a variety of stores, carrying packages of all shapes and sizes.

The pressure to consume, to have more and have it *right now* is real. And it drives many people to spend money they don't have, made easy with credit cards and loans. The resulting debt makes it difficult to keep up with payments and accumulated interest, and nearly impossible to save. With a heritage and culture like this, it's no wonder U.S. pet owners are plagued with financial difficulties.

An antidote to all this consuming is found in another age-old principle: contentment. Simply enjoy what you already have. Real satisfaction doesn't come from things, and satisfaction is different from enjoyment. While you might enjoy shopping, buying and acquiring, it won't bring long-term satisfaction. Honest. But you won't hear that from the advertisers. They don't want you to be satisfied. If you are, you won't buy a bigger, better, newer product.

Contentment, and the idea of making do with what you have, isn't new. Depression-era parents and grandparents know it well. As Wall writes, "This generation of savers devised a

SHOPPING TIP

Before the credit card, there was the layaway policy. Perhaps you've got your eye on a particular pet-care item. Pay a small amount down, have the retailer hold the goods and pay it off (usually interest-free—the advantage over credit cards) over a short period of time. Layaway policies vary, and some stores don't offer them, so be sure to ask.

sure-fire way to get everything they wanted: want less." It's an idea that needs reviving, and pet owners struggling to make ends meet will do well to adopt it. Be content with what you have for yourself—and for your pet. Be aware that just as the makers of clothing, electronics or autos want your business, so do pet product manufacturers. Don't be tempted to buy any or every new product that comes on the market. Make sure it's something the pet really needs, and make sure you have the money to acquire it.

Besides a cultural shift away from saving, people resist saving because it's perceived as painful. Saving is equated with being deprived, and once money is saved, that's the end of it. It vanishes into a dark hole never to be seen again. Nothing could be further from the truth. It's still your money, just set aside for a specific purpose (that you name). Saving money is not an end, but a means to an end: financial freedom.

What's potentially painful about saving is that it means *waiting* for something you need or want. It may take several months or even years to reach a financial goal, which is a very unpopular notion these days. We want everything right away: fast food, overnight mail delivery, instant credit. The idea of delaying gratification, even for a short time, is distasteful.

Having said all that, let's turn our attention to breaking the spending cycle and getting back to saving. Here are a few simple ways you can begin developing the savings habit. There's nothing difficult or really painful about these tips, so don't be afraid to read and implement them.

1. **Use the biblical principle of tithing.** It was once the custom to set aside one tenth of one's land or income to help support the church. You can use the same idea to take a portion right off the top of each paycheck and store it away. Do this before paying bills, pumping gas or buying kitty litter. This is important, because if you pay first and save what's left, you will never save. There's never anything left!

2. **Have someone else save for you.** If you can't be trusted to store away a portion yourself, have money removed from your paycheck or bank account and deposited into a savings account automatically through the company payroll deduction plan. What you don't see, you don't miss—and don't spend.

3. Save your next raise. Instead of planning how to spend the extra money, save it. The more money you earn, the more you should save.

4. Continue paying your debts. Even though you've just paid off your car, continue making payments, except pay them into a savings account.

5. Save grandma's checks. Do you receive small checks throughout the year from family members on birthdays or holidays? If so, don't cash them. Deposit them into your savings account.

6. Save all change. Those pennies, nickels and dimes eventually add up. Keep a jar handy and dump your change daily. At the end of the month, no matter how little, deposit it in your savings account.

7. Work overtime and bank the money. If time and family obligations permit, work a few extra hours each week with the intention of saving the extra earnings.

8. Set a goal. Don't think of a savings plan as a black hole. Give your savings a purpose, something special to work toward. If you want a pet, keep that in mind every time you save.

9. Cash only. It's amazing how simple this idea is, but it works. You will be less likely to part with money if you pay only in cash. It's odd, but checks and credit cards seem less like real money.

10. Make a sacrifice. Don't scream when you read this. A savings sacrifice doesn't need to be dramatic or life-threatening. Simply skip a lunch out this week with your work buddies, bring a sandwich and stash the money.

Your Savings Plan

You now understand how important it is to establish a personal savings program. Perhaps you're ready to actually stash some cash. Before slicing

open your pet's bed and stuffing it with $20s, though, you've got to estab-
lish a plan. Without a plan, you're like a ship lost at sea, tossed endlessly
with little idea where you're going. A savings plan, or goal, gives you a
direction and purpose for your money. It means you're in control of your
finances, not vice versa.

A savings plan can be as simple or complex, risky or safe, as you wish
it to be. You may have one goal or several. Some goals will be short-term,
some long-term. At first, it's probably best to keep your plan safe and
simple, especially if you're just kicking the spending habit and are prone to
backsliding.

Always remember that saving and investing money require know-how.
It's easy to get excited about the idea once you realize you really don't have
to be a slave to debt. You can win back your financial freedom. But don't
jump off the bridge until you've done your homework. There's much to
learn and you won't learn it all here. Instead, study the savings advice of
financial whizzes (see Chapter 10 for a list of books). Get the inside scoop
on specific ways to save and invest, compare them and think about it.
Consult with family members or friends who are experienced savers, and if
you know a trustworthy financial planner, ask for his or her advice. Each
financial goal must be carefully matched with specific savings plans. In
addition, goals should be reviewed and re-evaluated periodically. People
change, and so do their goals.

An *emergency fund* is a must, and is an excellent first savings goal for
pet owners. Recommendations vary, but financial experts generally advise
putting away enough money to cover living expenses for six months. This
will provide a cash reserve in case of illness, unemployment or unexpected
expenses (a huge veterinary bill, for example).

Where should you stash the emergency fund? Obviously, stuffing the
pet's bed really isn't a good idea. A regular savings account
(not great) or money market fund (better)
with a bank or credit union will suffice.
While you won't get much interest with
these accounts, the money is safe (in-
sured), easily accessible and there's

usually no withdrawal penalty. That's really important, too. An emergency fund is just that: a fund to be used in emergency. You have to be able to get your hands on it right away without penalties.

A *short-term savings plan*, money you'll need in six months to several years, is also important. This could cover your goal of adopting a pet in six months, private school tuition next year or buying a car in two. There are many types of accounts and investments that are appropriate for short-term saving, including certificates of deposit (CDs) or U.S. Treasury Bills. The advantage of these types of savings vehicles is that interest rates are higher than a regular or money market savings. The tradeoff is that you agree to keep the money invested for a specific time period.

A *long-term savings plan* is for money you won't need for more than five years. It may be difficult to think this far ahead, but if you're blessed with good health and manage to avoid catastrophe, you will grow old. Savings for the later years of life might include retirement or pension plans, or high-yield investments such as bonds or mutual funds.

This is a very basic re-introduction to the lost art of saving money. I encourage you to stop spending and implement a savings program right away. It's never too late. Next, read on to learn how to make the most of the money you do spend.

50 Simple Ways to Protect Your Hard-Earned Cash

1. Instead of going to a movie and spending money on admission, popcorn and drinks, take a stroll with your pet for free. Add the money you saved to your pet fund.

2. Save all your pocket change. Clean out pockets and purses at the end of each day and drop the coins in a jar. You'll be surprised how quickly pennies add up to dollars.

3. Recycle all your aluminum cans, plastic and glass bottles, newspaper, etc. Use the money from the deposits or from selling them for your pet-care costs.

4. Pack a lunch for work instead of eating out.

5. To save on utilities, use cold water settings on the washer and, in good weather, line-dry clothing.

6. Transfer high-interest credit card balances to one low-interest rate card.

7. Turn off lights in rooms that are not in use.

8. Don't let water run while washing dishes or brushing teeth, and take short showers.

9. Clip coupons for products you normally buy.

10. Buy in bulk.

11. Write letters instead of calling long distance. If you do call, pick up the telephone on nights and weekends, when the rates are lower.

12. Cancel magazine subscriptions. Read your favorite titles at the library instead.

13. Buy seasonal. Christmas decorations, for example, are usually on sale after the holiday. Buy next year's goods then.

14. Avoid convenience items, such as processed foods. Easy they are, but expensive.

15. In an effort to keep premiums to a minimum, some auto insurance companies work directly with customers by telephone or mail, eliminating an agent. Seek low-cost insurance for your vehicles and home.

16. Buy generic or store brands instead of name brands.

17. Mulch trees and shrubs to reduce watering.

18. Insulate your home properly.

19. Walk or ride a bike instead of driving.

20. Grow a vegetable garden and enjoy fresh, delicious veggies at minimal cost.

21. If you're entangled in a legal dispute and there isn't a large amount of money or property at stake, handle the problem yourself by taking it to small claims court.

22. If appropriate, ask for a senior, military or student discount.

23. Use 800 phone numbers whenever possible.

24. If your doctor approves, ask for the generic equivalent of medication.

25. Ask for a discount!

26. Buy vegetables in season from local growers. Not only are they fresh, but they're inexpensive.

27. Drop cable television service.

28. Purchase day-old bread.

29. Keep grocery and shopping bags and use them instead of store-bought trash bags.

30. Don't throw away old toothbrushes and sponges. Save for cleaning antiques, silverware or tennis shoes.

31. Drink powdered milk (if you really don't like the taste, mix it half and half with fresh milk, or use powdered only for cooking and baking).

32. Shop around for free or low-cost checking accounts. Many banks offer them free or with very low fees to loan customers or to those whose paychecks are deposited electronically. Beware of minimum balances, though, and charges associated with dropping below that balance.

33. Pay extra on your monthly mortgage. Banks are required to credit all extra payments directly to your principal, so this will reduce the time it takes to pay off the debt and reduce the amount of interest paid to the lender.

34. Buy greeting cards at thrift stores.

35. Carpool.

36. Professionals such as lawyers and accountants frequently offer free initial consultations or advice. Take advantage of it.

37. Shop department store clearance racks for low-cost, high-quality clothing.

38. During cold weather months, turn down the thermostat at night and snuggle up with an extra blanket and longjohns.

39. If you buy on credit, look for "interest free for the first six months" deals. Use with caution, though. Retailers are banking that you won't pay off the balance before the interest accrues; it's only a good deal if you pay off the balance.

40. Barter or swap for goods and services.

41. Beauty colleges and barber schools usually offer low-cost haircuts and other services. Check for a local school and give it a try.

42. Travel frequently? Consider joining a travel club. Yearly dues are required, but members receive hotel, dining, car rental and tour discounts.

43. Read invoices, such as hospital bills, credit cards and utility statements carefully. Mistakes do occur and you can be charged for services and goods you didn't ask for.

44. Many video stores have "free" shelves—videos you can rent for free.

45. Create a baby-sitting co-op.

46. Book off-season holidays. Depending upon the destination, you can save 10 to 50 percent on hotels, car rentals and other services.

47. Though it requires some labor, you can enjoy fruits and vegetables from your garden year-round by canning.

48. Save on restaurant meals by using diner discounts or weekly ads in the local paper.

49. Reuse paper products, such as large envelopes, computer paper or cardboard.

50. Instead of buying a date book, pick up a free one at a stationery store.

CHAPTER 6
Smart Shopping

The plans of the diligent lead surely to plenty, but those of everyone who is hasty, surely to poverty.
—Proverbs 21:5

Did you ever wonder why the pet industry is a billion-dollar business and why pet products sell so well? It's because today's owners consider their pets to be family members. They wish to love and nurture them, even spoil them a little, just as they might indulge a child. One way owners express fond feelings is by buying items for their pet: a special treat for bunny, a fun, colorful habitat for hamster, gourmet cookies for the dog or a tiny tent for the ferret.

Pets haven't always enjoyed family-member status. Not too many years ago the family dog was chained out back and fed table scraps; cats were allowed on the premises as long as they earned their keep by killing rodents; rabbits were skinned and eaten; mice were trapped and birds lived in the wild.

Society's change in attitude toward pets—from tolerated possessions to celebrated companions—is a good one, and is extremely positive for animals. It means, for most pets, a warm bed, regular meals, health care and love. The problem of homeless and abandoned pets is still with us. In general, though, pets are enjoyed and appreciated in the United States.

Which brings us to the pet industry. Manufacturers are well aware of the soft spot in owners' hearts for animal companions. They know owners want to offer pets the best of care, so they develop products to meet those needs; quality food, safe housing or items just for fun. There's nothing dark or evil about this; it's simply a matter of recognizing opportunity and capitalizing on it.

Happy Birthday!

According to a 1997 survey by the American Pet Products Manufacturers Association, 45 percent of all pet owners give gifts to their pets. Christmas and birthdays are the most common events for gift giving.

Dogs are most often the recipients of gifts: 66 percent of dog owners say they give their pets presents. Among both cat and bird owners, 54 percent give gifts to their pets. Forty-six percent of small animal owners give gifts, and 22 percent of fish and reptile owners do as well.

Many pet products on the market are essential; many aren't. To keep pet-care costs to a minimum, it is your responsibility to know the difference. But even more important, it's your responsibility to shop wisely.

Prudent shopping is a skill, according to the *Penny Pincher's Almanac*. Anyone can buy without thought, but shopping smart requires planning, research, knowing what you want and need and the ability to negotiate. The payoff is savings and reduced waste. Simply, if you shop carefully, you will reduce what you spend on pet care.

Amazingly, individuals who agonize over a large purchase such as a home, car or appliance, go soft when it comes to buying pet products. They buy impulsively. This is beneficial to retailers but it's not good for pet owners, especially those facing a financial squeeze. Again, showering pets with gifts is how some owners show affection. There's nothing wrong with that, but this heart factor can cloud clear thinking!

First and foremost, be a dedicated consumer when shopping for pet supplies. Don't let your guard down because you love your pet. Pets don't desire things, people do. Pets just want attention. Learn to shop wisely, which doesn't mean depriving your pet. It means saving money and getting the most for your pet-care dollar.

Once you've made a commitment to shop smart, you must take steps to learn how. Remember, prudent shopping is a skill. And like any skill, it requires effort and dedication to become proficient. Following are a few pointers on how to shop skillfully.

Research

One accomplished bargain hunter believes the key to getting the most for your money is to research the product. It's a belief that rings true. One of the biggest mistakes you can make is not researching the product or service you're about to pay for. Never *hope* to make a good choice. Educate yourself so you *know* it's a good choice. Train yourself to analyze everything you buy, and approach every purchase with an insatiable desire to learn everything you can about the product.

While this may sound more like obsession than prudent shopping, it isn't. It's being value-minded, according to William Roberts, author of *How to Save Money on Just About Everything*. The value-minded shopper takes time to learn about what he or she is buying.

Find out which manufacturers make the product. Identify individual features and/or differences. Who sells the product and for how much? Is there a warranty or other perks? Does the product live up to the manufacturer's claims? In short, become a student of the particular product you'd like to purchase. If you do, you'll pass your purchase exam with flying colors—guaranteed.

Evaluate

A prudent shopper gives careful consideration to what she needs, desires and can afford. Think carefully about what you'd like to buy and compare that to what you really need. Then factor in what you can spend. Think it over. Sleep on it a few nights. Then make an informed decision. Obviously, some purchases require more evaluation than others—items with a large price tag, for instance. But regardless of price, evaluate.

Know What You Need

This is an extension of the previous tip, but rather than thinking big, think small. What, specifically, do you need? What do you want? What's best for your pet? You can't expect to make a wise purchase if you can't answer these questions. Keep in mind that what you want isn't always what you need!

Compare

This is an extremely simple idea, but few people do it. While researching, you will learn probably more than you want to know about products. What do you do with that knowledge? Compare it! Compare products and compare prices. For example, flea dip A contains certain pesticides and costs a certain price for so many ounces. Examine flea dip B with the same bug killer for price and quantity. Is there a difference besides packaging? Which is the best buy?

It's fairly simple to compare a product such as flea dip, but some products require more thinking. Let's say you're in the market for electric pet clippers. Prices begin around $40 and go up to $200. There are several manufacturers that make numerous models. Some are made for home grooming, others for daily professional use. Some clippers have one-speed motors, some have two. Some are cordless, others aren't. The list of variables goes on and on. Selecting appropriate clippers isn't easy. You've got to know the products and understand their differences. You must know your own needs so you can choose. Once you've selected the features you need, you have a basis for comparing different makes and models.

Compare product prices store to store and shop where it's the most economical. Keep in mind that what's economical isn't always the lowest price. Suppose the cat litter you use is a few cents lower at a store 20 miles away, but available for pennies more a mile from your

SHOPPING TIP

Beware of cute, colorful items strategically placed by pet supply store cash registers. Called point-of-purchase items by retailers, these goodies are designed to catch your attention while standing in line. But before you toss the item in your basket, give it some thought. Chances are you really don't need it.

48

home. Obviously, it makes the most sense to purchase from the store near home. The money you spend on gas (which is getting more expensive every year!) driving to the other store offsets any savings.

Plan

Impulse buys are the result of not planning. A careful shopper plans, and impulse buys are not in her vocabulary. Once you've researched a product and thought about it, make a plan. When do you plan on buying it? Now, or in a few months? Do you have money, or do you plan to save or buy on credit? From whom are you planning to make the purchase, a pet supply store, a catalog company, another pet owner, or a secondhand shop? Map out a buying strategy and stay with it. This may seem like a sure way to kill the fun of impulsive shopping sprees—and it is. But it's a great way to save money.

Negotiate

Some people are natural-born hagglers, cutting deals—a peanut butter and jelly sandwich for a beloved toy—as early as kindergarten. They have a fabulous way of getting a better price, a better deal on just about anything. What do these hagglers know that the rest of us don't? *Everything is negotiable*.

In other words, don't take price tags at face value. An item may be marked $29.98, but it doesn't necessarily mean you have to pay that amount. A natural-born haggler sees a price tag as a challenge, an opportunity to negotiate. For the haggler, a price tag is the beginning of a deal, not the end.

The number one rule of the haggler is this: Ask for a discount. You don't know if you don't ask, right? You will be surprised at how often retailers will knock 10 to 20 percent off a price.

The haggler also knows who to ask for a discount. It's unlikely that a low-paid sales assistant has the authority to reduce a price. Ask to speak with the manager or owner.

If possible, buy in large quantities. The pet owner who buys several cases of pet food is more likely to receive a discount—providing she asks for it—than an owner buying six cans of food.

Credit cards are handy, but merchants who accept them pay a small fee (1 to 3 percent of the purchase price) to the credit card company. Offer to pay with greenbacks and ask for a cash discount.

Some people are downright uncomfortable with the idea of negotiating a price and feel as though doing so is rude or impolite. For the record, there's nothing impolite about negotiating. But hagglers must remember to

10 Foolproof Ways to Blow a Budget (Don't try this at home!)

1. Instead of adding to your pet savings fund, write yourself an IOU. Carry around the cash until the impulse to spend it is so overwhelming that you buy a coffeemaker you don't need.

2. Borrow $75 from your weekly grocery allowance to eat out one night.

3. Spend three weeks on holiday in the Cayman Islands.

4. Let bills stack up and accrue late charges.

5. Buy a costly item on a high-interest credit card, then pay only the minimum payment required each month. Watch those interest charges mount!

6. Call long distance and chat with old friends and relatives midday, midweek.

7. Turn all the lights on and take extra long, hot showers.

8. Keep a credit card handy while watching late night info-commercials.

9. Buy a boat.

10. Go shopping when you're upset or angry.

be polite and mannerly when making requests. A positive, cheerful attitude can mean money in your pocket.

Last, but not least, know the competitors' prices. Retailers want your business; they don't want you to walk out the door and buy somewhere else. If you let them know you can buy the same product somewhere else for less, you've got leverage for negotiating a better price.

CHAPTER 7
Why Preventive Care Saves Money

> *Real richness is in how you spend your money.*
>
> —Jacques Lipchitz

ne of the best, if not *the* best, ways to save money on pet care is to practice preventive care, says Janet Hornreich of the Humane Society of the United States. This is certainly not a new idea. But it's frequently overlooked.

Preventive care simply means providing a pet with care *before* something goes wrong. Vaccinations, for example, prevent life-threatening diseases. Obedience training helps prevent behavior problems that may prompt an owner to want to give up a dog. Routine flea control prevents tapeworm infestation—and misery! Proper nutrition keeps illness at bay.

If preventive care is so simple, why don't more pet owners practice it? One reason is that owners mistakenly believe spending money on routine care is wasteful. Why spend if there's nothing wrong? For instance, the kitten seems just fine, no sense in taking it to the vet and paying for an office visit as well as those expensive vaccinations. Who knows what tomorrow will bring? If a problem arises, that will be the time to shell out cash.

The problem with this type of thinking is that it leads to unnecessary suffering for the pet, and unnecessary heartache and expense for the owner.

The healthy kitten that doesn't receive vaccinations may not be healthy for long. It could be exposed to disease, fall desperately ill and require extensive veterinary treatment to recover. A hospital stay and treatment aren't cheap, either. The money saved by not vaccinating is lost three-fold. And there's a chance that despite the treatment, the kitten won't recover. The moral of the story? Prevent suffering. Spend now. It's really less expensive in the long run.

Here's a preventive care checklist. Have you considered the following preventive measures?

Collar and Tags

The primary reason shelters are unable to return lost pets to owners is because the animals are not wearing collars and current identification tags. Avoid the heartache of never having a pet returned, should it happen to slip out the back gate, by making sure all pets wear well-fitting collars with tags. It's certainly not a large investment—maybe $10 for a collar and $5 for a tag—but it can save millions in heartache later on.

Deworming

Internal parasites are nasty buggers that can wreak havoc on the health of a pet. Parasites such as tapeworms, whipworms or roundworms make their living by growing and multiplying in a host's body. Initially, the animal seems fine, but in time, an infested animal becomes ill, anemic and robbed of vital nutrients.

A routine check for internal parasites is simple, and tells whether or not the animal is hosting unwelcome visitors. The veterinarian checks the animal's fecal matter under a microscope, usually as part of the annual exam, to determine which parasites, if any, are present. If parasites are present, medication is prescribed. And that's usually the end of it.

Don't make the mistake of thinking indoor pets can't get internal parasites. They can! Make sure a fecal exam is part of the pet's yearly vet visit.

Even if the animal looks healthy, it could be harboring internal parasites, which, in time, will make their unwelcome presence known.

Diet

Your mother was right: If you don't eat all your vegetables, and other nutritious foods, you won't be healthy. The same is true for pets of all species. Proper diet is essential to good health. Consult with a veterinarian—at the yearly checkup is a good time—to plan your pet's menu. Following that, use common sense. Feed a balanced diet, limit treats and offer fresh, clean water at all times.

A note of caution: In an attempt to cut costs, be careful not to purchase low-quality foods. Some veterinarians advise owners to stick with name brand or premium foods; avoid generic. This way, you can be assured of quality and save money, too. That's because generic foods only *seem* cheaper. In reality, premium foods are the better buy. It costs less per serving to feed a quality diet because more nutritional value is packed into a smaller amount. Look at how much food the manufacturer recommends daily for your pet. With the premium foods the amount is much less. You can compare the cost per day of equal-weight bags of food by noting on your calendar what you spent for the food and then tracking how long it lasts.

What's for Dinner?

According to a 1997 survey by the American Pet Products Manufacturers Association, 69 percent of dog owners feed their pets dry dog food and 6 percent feed canned dog food. Among cat owners, 93 percent buy dry food and 63 percent buy canned food. For fish owners, 93 percent feed food flakes, and 31 percent feed food pellets. Almost all bird owners buy seed, most often in boxes, and 31 percent also give their birds vitamins or supplements. Among reptile owners, 31 percent feed live food, including rodents, crickets and other insects, while 42 percent feed fruits and vegetables and 41 percent opt for a dry formula reptile diet.

Generally, dry foods are less expensive than canned, and most animals do fine on them. Just make sure they get plenty of water. Semi-moist are the most expensive, but they are not always the best. Make sure you compare ingredients, and look at the nutritional analysis on the food label.

Also, some owners purchase foods in bulk to save money. However, vitamins tend to degrade during storage. Don't buy more than your pet will eat in a month and store it in a cool, dry place such as a garbage can with a tight-fitting lid. Be sure to store avian seed mixes in containers with tight-fitting lids. If you wish to buy in bulk, share the purchase with another pet owner.

Advocates for homemade diets believe that fresh, raw foods are the best preventive measure an owner can offer his or her pet. While the expense may be higher initially, it's less in the long run because the pet is healthy. Before you switch your pet to a homemade diet, make sure you learn enough about its nutritional needs to be able to feed a complete and balanced diet.

Serve only fresh fruit and vegetables (some owners include fresh frozen) to birds, small mammals and reptiles. Some reptiles and most amphibians require live food, which must be purchased as needed, unless you plan to raise it at home.

Besides a healthy diet, some animals require something extra. Rabbits, for instance, need hay to add roughage to their diet. Seed-eating birds need grit to help break down their food and cuttlebone to supply calcium. Small mammals often require vitamin supplements in their water, as do reptiles. Study the nutritional needs of your individual pet species, and provide it with an appropriate diet. The result will be nothing less than good health.

Environment

Along with a proper diet, pets require a proper environment to prevent problems. This isn't as essential with dogs and cats as it is with reptiles and amphibians, small mammals and birds. Dogs and cats fit nicely into the owner's habitat, which is why they're commonly called housepets. Reptiles and amphibians, however, do not. Owners must create artificial environments for these species that simulate as closely as possible the creature's natural habitat. Air temperature and humidity must be just right, as well as lighting and hiding places.

Small mammals must be confined in safe, interesting enclosures that allow them to express normal behaviors such as chewing or scurrying through a burrow. Birds must be housed, at least part of the time, in safe enclosures that make them feel secure, yet give them enough room to exercise.

This isn't as easy as it seems, especially for reptiles and amphibians. Know your particular species and plan an appropriate habitat. An improper environment can stress the animal, leading to illness or death.

Exercise

The fat plague that affects many people also affects their pets, and so do the health problems associated with obesity. Avoid this! Make sure pets eat right and get plenty of exercise.

House small mammals in roomy cages and supply them with exercise wheels, toys and tunnels to keep busy. Leash train your rabbit and stroll around the neighborhood. Encourage the feline species to get moving by tossing catnip toys, climbing trees (indoors) or retrieving wads of paper.

Exercise requirements differ among canine breeds, so plan activities accordingly. Doberman Pinschers, for example, are high-energy dogs that enjoy a quick game of fetch. A brisk walk around the block may suffice for a dainty Toy Poodle.

As with any activity, begin slowly, especially if the animal is overweight, to avoid injury. If exercise is part of a weight-reduction program, follow the veterinarian's suggestions. The health benefits of exercise are countless, for both you and your pet. And perhaps best of all, it's a fun way for you both to spend time together.

Flea Control

Considered an external parasite, fleas are probably at the top of owners' Most Hated lists. Not only are they a biting-itching-scratching irritant, but

SHOPPING TIP

Did you ever wonder why retailers display items? It's because they realize that if consumers see how something looks, works or is to be used, they're more likely to buy it. Buy only what you need, not what appears

they can also cause health problems. A heavily infested pet can become anemic from all the biting and blood sucking. It can also become infested with tapeworms, which are carried by the flea to the pet's digestive system when the pet chews an itch and swallows a flea. Fleas also carry other types of diseases and parasites that can end up in your pet's bloodstream.

Some animals are allergic to the flea's bite, which results in flea bite dermatitis, an itchy skin condition that is pure misery for the pet. It's also difficult to manage and can be expensive to treat.

While fleas do not make life miserable for all animal species, they must be controlled—if for no other reason than that they also bite humans. Spray the yard, fog and vacuum the house, bathe and dip the pet. Consider internal flea control. Several new products are now available that can break the flea lifecycle without causing harm to your pet. Talk to your veterinarian about them.

The best products on the market now are usually the most expensive, but also the least toxic to you and your pet. There is no question, however, that avoiding dangerous toxins is worth the money. It's certainly not easy to keep fleas at bay, and good flea-control products are expensive. However, money invested in flea control is money well spent.

Grooming

A bath, brush and/or trim will do wonders for a pet's appearance, but that's not the only reason to groom regularly. It's healthy. Brushing is good for a pet's skin: It increases circulation, removes dead hair and skin and promotes oil production. Brushing during times of heavy shedding also reduces the chances the animal will ingest hair and develop fur balls.

Grooming gives an owner (or professional groomer) the opportunity to look the pet over from head to tail. Look for lumps or bumps, slightly red ears or a tender foot. Such subtle signs could be an indication of illness—and the earlier it's noticed and treated, the better.

Frequent bathing for dogs and cats is a good idea during flea season to get rid of the pests and soothe an itching pet. Regular bathing helps reduce a ferret's strong, natural odor. Rabbits and guinea pigs should only be bathed if absolutely necessary, but regular brushing is a must. Hamsters, mice and gerbils require almost no grooming; they bathe themselves. So do birds and reptiles, but you must make sure they have plenty of clean water in the right kind of container to take the kind of bath or shower they need.

Dogs, especially, need their toenails trimmed regularly. A long, curled toenail can be painful. Rabbits and other small mammals need nails trimmed, too, or their long, soft nails can catch and tear. Regular teeth brushing, along with a hard kibble diet, for dogs and cats will prevent dental disease.

Heartworm Preventives

The bad news is heartworm disease commonly affects dogs, and has been reported in people and other animals. It is spread by the ordinary mosquito and can be found wherever mosquitoes breed. Infection begins when larvae from an infected mosquito are deposited in the animal's skin. They burrow into the animal, and eventually develop into adult worms. The worms make their way to a vein, move to the right side of the heart and mature, interfering with the function of the heart.

A pet infested with heartworms is a sick pet, indeed. Hospitalization is required, and the outcome is not always positive. The good news is medication is available to prevent heartworms. It is given orally every day or once a month, and works by killing heartworm larvae before they mature.

Obviously, giving a pet heartworm preventive makes good sense, especially if you live in an area prone to mosquito infestation.

Immunizations

The sad fact about neglecting to vaccinate pets against disease is that a pet's suffering can be prevented. Young animals receive a series of shots that build immunity, then yearly boosters, usually as part of the annual checkup, thereafter to keep defenses up. It's really that simple. Failing to do so can result in illness, expense, even death. Be kind to your pet. Vaccinate every year, or as recommended by your vet.

Not all animal species require vaccinations, so be sure to learn whether or not your pet needs to be immunized. Ferrets, for example, must be protected against canine distemper, which is fatal to them, as well as rabies. Vaccinations are required by law for some animal species, in some states and cities.

License

State and local ordinances vary, but some pets must be licensed. (Whether you agree with that is beside the point—while you are working to change the law, you still must obey it.) The benefit to following such ordinances is that the animal usually must be vaccinated against rabies to obtain a license. This obviously prevents an outbreak of a deadly, costly illness. Not buying a license can result in more expense if owners are fined for not complying.

A license is also an effective way to identify your pet, should it ever become lost.

Routine Checkups

A lot of owners neglect their pet's yearly exam, but a regular going over by a knowledgeable veterinarian is one of the best ways to detect illness early on. And detecting a health problem right away, before it has a chance to cause extensive damage, is best for the pet and less expensive for the owner. Ear mites in a rabbit, for instance, could be undetectable to a novice owner but noticeable to a vet examining an ear closely, and treatment is fairly simple. Letting the ear fester without treatment means suffering for the animal and more extensive treatment later on (which translates into more money).

Take full advantage of a yearly vet visit. You are paying for the veterinarian's time, so use it. Write down any questions you may have, perhaps about feeding or behavior. Ask the vet to show you how to clip toenails or clean ears. Ask about simple signs of illness or recommendations for flea control.

While most veterinarians are very busy people, if a vet seems too busy to answer questions or brushes off your concerns, find another vet. There are plenty of caring, sensitive vets who want nothing more than to help owners care for pets properly and cost-effectively.

Safety

A rabbit chews on an electrical cord and burns its mouth. A curious kitten licks an open bottle of antifreeze and loses it life. A flying bird crashes into a sliding glass door. Traumatic incidents such as these can be prevented, and so can the heartache and expense that goes along with them. Prevent accidents in your home by making it safe for pets. Just as parents of wandering toddlers baby-proof the house and yard to prevent accidents, so must pet owners pet-proof their environment. Simple steps, such as keeping medicines or cleaning products locked away, or removing dangling electrical cords, will go a long way toward preventing accidents. Following that, supervision is essential, as well as escape-proof enclosures.

Spay or Neuter

If you take anything to heart in this book, let it be this: Spay or neuter your pet. Altering a pet surgically so it can no longer reproduce is the ultimate cost-cutter, especially with dogs, cats, rabbits and ferrets. Altered pets are happier, better-adjusted pets and they do not produce litters and litters of unwanted young. The health benefits of neutering pets have also been well-documented. They include lower incidences of certain cancers and infections. There are no down-sides here.

Training

The number one reason pets are dumped at shelters by their owners is behavior problems. Owners are frustrated, overwhelmed or fed up with the dog's digging, the cat's spraying, the rabbit's biting. Instead of working to solve a problem, they figure it's best to relinquish the animal. The problem with this is it isn't fair to the animal and it doesn't solve anything. It only creates more trouble: a grim, stressful future for the pet and an ill-informed owner who will probably acquire another pet and be faced with more of the same behavior issues.

Training can be the perfect solution when behavior problems emerge. Better yet, training can prevent them! Early, consistent training and socialization go a long way toward shaping a young animal's mind—positively. The animal learns acceptable behavior and is rewarded for it. It may never learn bothersome habits that would otherwise leave it homeless in a shelter. If it does have bad habits, kind, consistent training can correct them.

Early and continued training will also save on replacement costs for chewed up furniture; stain and odor removers for carpet soiling; legal fees if the animal bites someone; and personal frustration.

CHAPTER 8

Tips for Beginner Bargain Hunters

> *A bargain is something you have to find a use for once you have bought it.*
> —Ben Franklin

Who doesn't love a bargain? What a thrill for a dedicated bargain hunter to find a prized item at a greatly reduced price. Think of how much money you've saved! Finding a bargain is fun, exciting, even addicting.

But one thing about bargains: They don't come knocking on your door. They are elusive creatures found when you least expect it (which makes finding one even more exciting). Bargain hunting is just that: a hunt. It requires searching, seeking, planning. You must be creative and patient, and you must search for bargains just as a detective might search for clues.

Here are some leads for chasing down pet-care bargains. Happy hunting!

Catalogs

Mail order prices are frequently less than retail prices. Check out the classified sections in animal publications; they're loaded with ads for pet supply catalogs. (If you don't subscribe to a pet magazine, visit the local library.) Most catalogs are free and can be ordered by calling the company's 800 number.

There's just one thing to beware of when you're catalog shopping: the shipping and handling charges. If you're just buying a few inexpensive items, those charges can quickly blow a bargain. Always add up the charges before you decide to buy. And, because bigger orders tend to get a better deal on shipping and handling, save up your orders, or order together with other pet-owning friends.

Coupons

Coupon lovers are already savvy, but for those left out of the loop, look for pet food coupons inside food bags, on the back of bags and behind can labels. Don't expect a big savings, but every penny does count. Be on the lookout for "junk" mailings, and watch for coupons wrapped up in the Sunday newspaper.

Local pet supply stores often mail out flyers to encourage business. For example, grooming for half price with a coupon or a bag of food at 20 percent off. Breeders and pet supply stores sometimes provide clients with coupons for food or products, as do humane organizations. Be sure to ask when you get your pet.

Coupon cutting and saving isn't for everyone. As one busy dog-cat-bird owner says, "It's just too much trouble." But for those willing to cut coupons, it can cut costs.

Estate Sales

An estate sale is a high-end garage sale that takes place after someone has died. The deceased person's home and furnishings are sold; sales are usually managed by professionals, especially if there are a lot of valuables. If the deceased individual was a pet owner, you may be able to pick up such items as feeding dishes, a dog house, an aquarium or pet books.

Estate sale prices are usually fixed, but it can't hurt to ask for a discount. To locate a sale, look in the classified section of the newspaper

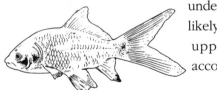

under "Estate Sales" for listings. You're most likely to find nice items at sales in wealthy, upper-class neighborhoods, so plan accordingly.

Free Samples

Who doesn't enjoy something free? They're difficult to find, and certainly not predictable, but free samples from pet food and product manufacturers are always fun to receive. Pet trade shows open to the public are a great place for freebies. Manufacturers display their wares and usually give away product samples, small packets of food and informative brochures. Trade shows open to the public are usually advertised on local television stations and in newspapers. Watch for ads. You may also find free offers on coupons or in magazine or newspaper advertisements. Take advantage of any giveaway offer you find. After all, it's free!

Garage Sales

A favorite American activity, garage sales are great places to find treasures others consider trash, or at least unwanted stuff. Garage sales are advertised in the classified section of the newspaper; ads frequently include bits of information about what's for sale, so look for pet supplies. Sales are usually held on Friday, Saturday and Sunday.

If garage sales are your fancy, be sure to rise early. Most begin at 8 a.m. and the good stuff goes quickly. Prices are variable at garage sales, so even if an item is marked with a price, go ahead and offer less. Most people are flexible, especially on Sunday. If it doesn't sell, it has to be packed up and put back in the garage. If you don't see pet supplies available, ask. Chances are there's an unused rabbit hutch sitting in the backyard.

Magazine Advertisements

Animal publications are a great place to find classified and display listings of everything from antiques and collectibles to flea-control products to animal-care books to free health information. Be aware that ads, while extensive and specific, do not necessarily tout discounted pet products or services.

Membership Warehouses

These oversized membership markets from which no one can exit without spending at least $100 are very popular, and for good reason. Not only can you buy anything from appliances to clothing to groceries, but you can buy it cheap. That goes for pet food, too, and sometimes pet supplies.

There are a few disadvantages, though. You won't always find the same products each time you shop. Pet foods frequently change; one month the brand of dog food you usually buy is available, while the next month it isn't. Not only is this inconvenient, but it can spell digestive upset for a pet. Switching foods should be avoided. Also, you must be a member. Check with individual warehouses for membership requirements.

Military Bases

If you're serving in the armed forces, you are familiar with the base commissary. A commissary is a store operated for base personnel. It is not open to the public. As a perk to military members and families, prices are usually below retail. By purchasing pet food and supplies on base, you may be

Where to Shop?

Where do most Americans shop for their pets? A survey by the American Pet Products Association found the most common outlets for dog and cat food purchases are grocery and discount stores. Fish food, bird food and reptile food are purchased most often at traditional pet supply stores or discount stores.

Maintenance items like vitamins are purchased for dogs most often in discount outlets or at a veterinarian's office. Cat maintenance products are typically bought at grocery stores and discount stores. Traditional pet supply stores were the main outlet for fish, bird, small animal and reptile maintenance products.

Accessories for dogs and cats, such as leashes and collars, are generally purchased at discount stores. Accessories for fish, small animals and reptiles are more often purchased at pet supply stores or discount outlets.

Cat, dog and bird owners buy their pets' toys mainly at discount stores, followed by traditional pet supply stores.

able to reduce costs. Check individual base stores for the availability of pet-related items.

Newspaper Advertisements

Some people looking to sell animal-related items advertise in the newspaper classified section under "Pets and Supplies." Mini-ads, sometimes called "Thrifties," are another section to check. Many advertisers sell equipment along with animals; call to find out.

Pet Supply Superstores

The small, neighborhood mom-and-pop pet supply store can still be found, but large superstores are the future of pet supplies. These giants not only stock supplies for all companion animals, but frequently have a grooming salon, veterinary clinic and pet adoption center. Selection is plentiful, prices competitive. Look in the local newspaper for sales, coupons and specials. Some stores offer discounts on products or services when you adopt a pet.

Sales

Watch for retailer sales and specials, which may be advertised in newspapers, on the radio or on television. Or, you may receive a flyer in the mail. New products are sometimes discounted when introduced; other products are discounted periodically. Take advantage of specials by stocking up on discounted items that you know you'll always need, such as kitty litter or bedding for a small mammal.

SHOPPING TIP

In response to consumer demand and a more sophisticated pet-owning public, pet supply store staff members are better trained and more knowledgeable about caring for pets. Take advantage of this. Ask sales assistants questions about individual species or items, or ask for a demonstration of a product. However, don't feel obligated to buy just because you asked for assistance.

Swap Meets or Flea Markets

Swap meets, which are usually held outdoors on Saturday and Sunday mornings, are a fun experience and a great place for a bargain. Vendors, basically anyone who has stuff to sell, congregate in large parking lots, selling everything (used and new) from fruit to baby clothing to tools. You'll see all kinds of treasures and all kinds of interesting people selling them.

New items are usually less than retail price, so if you happen upon a vendor selling pet supplies, check the prices. Bargaining is the name of the game here, so don't be shy. And don't pay too much.

Like garage sales, swap meets open early and the good stuff goes fast. Arrive on time so you don't miss the best items.

Tack and Feed Stores

Most prevalent in rural communities (and often the only place to buy pet products), tack and feed stores sometimes sell pet food in bulk. Don't expect a wide selection of products, but prices are usually reasonable.

Thrift Stores

One person's trash is another's treasure. Frequently a fund-raising device for nonprofit organizations, thrift stores are filled with a wide variety of used, donated goods, including pet supplies. Don't expect to find collars, leashes or toys, but kennel crates, feeding dishes, glass aquariums, egg crate foam (for bedding) and pet books are common finds.

You can never be sure what you'll find in a thrift store—which is half the fun of shopping in one—so don't have your heart set on finding a specific item at a specific store on a specific day. Browse several stores in town each week; most stores receive new (old) merchandise weekly. Look in the Yellow Pages to find thrift stores in your area.

Thrift stores usually price each item, so don't expect to bargain. Many have senior discount days (Tuesdays, for example), or special tag days (items with blue tags, for instance, are half price on Fridays). Shop carefully. Items are sold "as is" and cannot be returned.

Two Commonsense Ideas

You can reduce your pet-care budget by being willing to improvise and use items that aren't brand new. These aren't new ideas, just practical, commonsense ones.

A Few Cautions

After shopping at thrift stores or garage sales, there's something you're sure to notice: Many items are flawed, slightly damaged, broken or missing something. And that goes for any pet supplies you might find. The otherwise perfect plastic kennel crate door is ajar, the ceramic feeding bowl is slightly chipped or the iguana care book is missing its cover. Expect such imperfections. Don't overlook them, though, and keep them in perspective with the price tag. If it can't be fixed or is potentially dangerous, it's not a good buy, no matter the price.

Clean all secondhand items carefully before using them, to minimize any chance of illness or infection. Wash in a dishwasher or wash and sanitize with chlorine bleach, and then rinse very thoroughly. To lessen the risk of injury, make any necessary repairs before allowing a pet to use an item.

Improvise

Sure, it's nice to be able to walk into a store and buy what you want, when you want it, regardless of cost. Few people can do that, though. So if you're like the majority of the population that must stick to a budget, improvise—make do with what you have to save money.

For example, you need plastic bags to pick up feces when you walk your dog. You can buy special bags, mitts and kits made just for dogs—which are great if you can pay the price. You don't have to pay the price, though. Use a plastic grocery bag. It's free (after you buy the groceries), easy to get and does the job.

While it's certainly easiest and most convenient to buy items made specifically for an animal species, it's certainly not the least expensive way to do it. For example, one manufacturer sells a play yard that is handy for confining a dog. The product is marketed to dog owners, but the manufacturer also markets the same product to parents of very young children—at a lower cost.

Check out the product you're interested in. Is it made specifically for a rabbit, or is it also made for other animals, or another purpose, and sold for less?

Used Items

Some people have an aversion to used items, others don't. Don't be afraid to use secondhand pet-care items, as long as they're in good condition. There's no shame in it, and your pet doesn't care.

CHAPTER 9
100 Thrifty Ideas

> *You cannot bring about prosperity by discouraging thrift.*
> —Abraham Lincoln

Reducing pet-care costs isn't just counting pennies. It's an attitude, a way of life. It's a creative mind-set that saves, improvises, substitutes or is willing to wait. Unfortunately, being thrifty, the art of practicing economy and good management, seems to be unpopular, even forgotten. Today, many people are in such a hurry to acquire things that they don't bother to compare prices, wait for sales or really think about a purchase. Credit cards make it easy to buy, now, and perhaps beyond your means.

The American Dream of financial success—the promise of equal opportunity for all who are willing to work hard and bide their time—has been replaced with a flurry of credit spending, with little attention to savings and plain old common sense. The most obvious symptom of this dream gone bad, writes Rochelle LaMotte McDonald in *How to Pinch a Penny Till It Screams,* is our huge national debt.

It's time to stop overspending. As unpopular as the notion might be, especially to pet supply manufacturers and retailers, instead of heading to the pet supply store every time you need something, stop and think. Ask yourself:

✂ Is this item really necessary?

✂ Can I make it myself?

✂ What supplies might be necessary and where can they be purchased?

✂ Would it cost less to make it than it would to buy it?

✂ Do I have the time, and am I willing, to do it myself?

✂ Can I use something I already have at home?

✂ Is what I'm substituting safe for my pet?

✂ Is it something I need right away, or can I wait and save to buy it?

✂ Have I shopped around for the best price?

If you can make it yourself for less money than you can buy it, do it. If you don't need it right away, wait until it goes on sale. If you haven't compared prices, do so. If you have a safe substitute at home, use it. Remember, if you take time to think carefully about purchases and services, you will reduce pet-care costs, especially if you resist buying impulsively.

Another thought: Don't be afraid to make use of items that are not marketed specifically for pets. For example, use a pie plate or paper plate to feed the cat instead of buying a special cat dish. The cat dish may be cuter, but it's also far more expensive. The pie plate sitting in a cupboard at home will work just as well, and there's no added expense. It's not as fun, but the cat doesn't care. Pet products are not marketed to animals, they are marketed to the people who own them. Don't feel as though you have to buy or use products labeled for pets if there's a low-cost, safe substitute available.

That's not to say products made specifically for pets do not have their place. They do, and today's owners are fortunate to be able to

SHOPPING TIP

Try "dry" shopping. Leave your money and credit cards at home and simply take a stroll through a local pet supply store. Think about what products you might like to buy and why. Make a list afterward and think about it.

purchase items that were not available just a few years ago. However, owners need not feel compelled to always buy such products. Give some thought to the product you're considering. Then make a decision.

Following are 100 simple, commonsense ideas that can help lower pet care costs. Obviously, this list is only the beginning. Use your imagination and create new ways to save.

1. If you own several pets of the same species and they'll eat together without fur flying, serve dinner in a trough—a 9 × 13–inch baking dish.

2. Build a rabbit hutch.

3. Grow an organic garden. Plant vegetables to feed a bird, reptile, rabbit or guinea pig, or add to the dog's homemade diet.

4. Instead of buying an expensive orthopedic bed for an arthritic, elderly dog, make a bed from egg crate foam and several washable blankets. Foam and blankets are cheap and easy to find at thrift stores. Simply lay the foam down and cover with folded blankets.

5. Instead of custom furniture covers made just for families with pets, buy inexpensive slip covers from a discount store.

6. Recycle plastic grocery bags by using them to pick up feces while walking the dog.

7. Make a cat toy by crumpling a clean, plain sheet of paper. Toss and watch the action begin!

8. Tie a knot in a heavy, athletic sock and *violà*—a puppy toy.

9. Grow a batch of catnip in a flower pot or window box.

10. Make a bed for kitty with a towel and a cardboard box. The towel should be soft and washable; the box about four inches high.

11. Use kitchen-size garbage bags to line the litter box instead of buying special liners.

12. Adopt a pet from a shelter or rescue organization. Fees are minimal, and shelter pets are usually altered and immunized.

13. Buy shampoo, conditioner and flea dip in gallons, rather than eight-ounce bottles. It's less expensive, ounce for ounce.

14. Join a breed or species club. Dues are usually minimal, and friendly, informative resources plentiful.

15. Check out the library for pet-related books, magazines and videos.

16. Search "$5 stores" or discount bookstores for pet books, calendars and videos.

17. Don't toss old towels. Keep for after-bath drying, beds or cleaning up messes.

18. Instead of pouring shampoo directly from a bottle onto the pet, dilute the shampoo in a small bucket and apply with a sponge. Diluting stretches the shampoo and using a sponge gets more onto the pet and less down the drain.

19. Carpet samples and scraps are handy pet beds, although they can be difficult to keep clean. Cover with a washable towel. Carpet samples also make great scratching pads for cats.

20. A plain cardboard box makes a great hideaway for a bunny. Place inside the hutch and change frequently—rabbits are chewers. Make sure the box doesn't have sticky tape that the rabbit could ingest.

21. Store pet food in a plastic garbage can with a tight-fitting lid to keep it fresh.

22. Invest in a good veterinary medical book and follow home care advice. Many minor conditions can be treated at home by an owner, eliminating the expense of unnecessary veterinary visits. Don't substitute a book for good veterinary care, though, and be sure to consult with a vet when in doubt.

23. Word of mouth is the best kind of help for owners facing a financial crunch. Ask friends and relatives who own pets how they solved particular problems or saved on pet care costs.

24. Give a bunny a paper plate and watch the fun. Rabbits love to toss them in the air.

25. Check out the Internet. Rates for online services vary, but many charge one low fee each month. For that rate, you can be in touch with hundreds of pet-related forums, clubs and news groups, which provide you with simple veterinary advice, training tips, help locating a specific type of pet and friendships with other pet owners. You'll also find electronic pet supply shops with hundreds of available items. (Check prices carefully.)

26. Call a pet-food manufacturer's toll-free number for basic nutritional information and advice; free written materials are often available upon request.

27. Instead of hiring a professional groomer, groom your pet at home or at a self-service pet wash.

28. Locate a low-cost spay/neuter or immunization clinic. Call local shelters for dates and times of upcoming clinics.

29. Does your dog need a sweater? Instead of buying canine clothing, improvise with a T-shirt. Use baby and child-size T-shirts for small dogs, adult-size T-shirts for large breeds. Or pick up an old baby sweater at a thrift shop.

30. If a veterinarian prescribes medication for your pet, before paying for the prescription ask her if she has samples. Or find out if the medication is available over-the-counter. If so, it may be less expensive to buy it at a discount drugstore.

31. If your pet is sprayed by a skunk, soak it in tomato juice rather than buying odor remover. Unfortunately, there is no magic cure—other than time—for skunk odor, no matter what manufacturers claim. Tomato juice works just as well as commercial products.

32. Once-a-day tablet and liquid heartworm preventives are less expensive than once-a-month preventives. However, many owners don't wish to be bothered with medicating a pet every day. Instead of buying a preventive from a veterinarian, order it from a veterinary supply catalog such as KV Vet Supply (800-423-8211) or Foster and Smith (800-826-7206). To order, you must include a veterinarian's prescription. Also, the animal must test negative for heartworms. Medicating an infested pet is deadly.

33. Consider alternative veterinary treatments. While an office visit for a holistic vet may cost the same, treatments such as herbal medicine are usually less expensive than pharmaceuticals.

34. Barter. Try swapping services for services. For example, perhaps you're a carpenter experiencing a slump, but the vet needs some repairs at his clinic. Offer to trade services.

35. Recycle newspapers by using them to line the litter box or paper train a pup.

36. Plastic pet food can covers are a common promotional giveaway, especially at shelters. Ask for one.

37. Use mild baby shampoo to bathe a ferret rather than shampoo made just for ferrets.

38. Save vegetable scraps: carrot tops and peelings, radish tops, broccoli stems, etc. Feed to rabbits, birds and other veggie-loving pets. Make sure they're fresh, though, and don't overfeed.

39. Clean and disinfect pet areas and dishes with ordinary bleach and water rather than expensive household or "pet" cleaners. Be sure to rinse well and let dry thoroughly before allowing your pet access.

40. Keep cats and rabbits indoors and dogs in a fenced yard to protect them from injuries, such as being hit by a car. This simple idea will prevent the expense of emergency vet care, as well as the heartbreak of an injured pet.

41. Form a neighborhood puppy training club. If paying for puppy training classes is out of the question, check out a few training books and videos from the library and gather up a group of friends and neighbors who have pups. Get together to practice obedience lessons and help pups become accustomed to other dogs. Consult with other experienced owners when problems and questions arise.

42. Feed your pet a good-quality dry food, which is less expensive than canned or semi-moist. Mix in a little canned food to encourage a finicky eater.

43. Brush a little baking soda through a ferret's coat to deodorize.

44. Don't buy commercially prepared ear cleaners. Instead, wipe out a pet's ears with a 50-50 mixture of rubbing alcohol and hydrogen peroxide, or use mineral oil or witch hazel.

45. No need to buy a specially made bird cage cover. Simply cover the cage at night with a large towel or blanket.

46. Make your own pet treats. Pet treat recipes abound, so pick one that sounds yummy and get in the kitchen.

47. To untangle your pet's fur, instead of buying a commercial detangler sprinkle a bit of cornstarch on the mats, then brush them out gently.

48. Save empty toilet paper and paper towel rolls. Gerbils and hamsters love them!

49. Crate train your pup. Not only do dogs enjoy their own private den, but crating helps prevent soiling in the house.

50. Plastic water bottles for small mammals tend to crack and split with time. When this happens, don't throw away the drinking nozzle. Make a new bottle by screwing the nozzle onto a clean plastic soda bottle.

51. Dab a little Avon Skin-So-Soft bath oil onto your freshly washed dog. It repels fleas!

52. Attend low-cost pet obedience, care or grooming seminars sponsored by local humane organizations.

53. Keep bird seed fresh by storing in clean mayonnaise or peanut butter jars.

54. Don't toss aluminum foil. Make a pet food can lid by folding together several sheets.

55. Make a house for a small mammal with a child-size shoe box.

56. Instead of buying a cover-up, wear an old, oversized button-down shirt when toting a bird on your shoulder.

57. Make a training "rattle can" with an empty soda can. Drop in a few small pebbles and tape shut the opening.

Do-It-Yourself Safety

Some skilled owners are determined to build housing for their pets. Not only can this save money, but it's fun. To ensure the iguana cage or aviary will be safe, consider the following:

- Use quality material. It's okay to economize, but don't skimp.

- Use safe material. Beware of paints, preservatives, sharp wire or nails.

- Build the cage so it is escape-proof.

- Plan! Check out a book from the library or request building plans on the Internet. Think over the project carefully with your pet's safety in mind. Sketch out a plan and estimate the cost of materials before you build.

- Before introducing your pet to its custom-built home, check it carefully. For example, do all the latches work properly? Are there any loose nails or stray bits of wire?

58. Fill an inexpensive spray bottle with water to make a kitty training device or an avian bath spray.

59. Buy small mammal bedding in bulk.

60. Make the most of yearly vet visits. Ask questions; have the vet or assistant show you how to clip wings, toenails, etc.

61. Make a pet first-aid kit instead of buying one. Ask your vet what you need, then assemble the items yourself.

62. Pet supply store clerks are usually well informed about particular species. Ask for advice.

63. If you buy more than one pet identification tag, companies often offer a slight price break. Even if you have only one pet, order extra tags. Keep them in case of loss.

64. Swap pet-sitting services with a friend.

65. Call humane organizations for care or behavior advice.

66. Check "Pets and Supplies" in the classified section of the newspaper for "free to good home" pets.

67. Pick up manufacturers' free care brochures at pet supply stores.

68. Make your own pet food scoop. Cut a plastic milk jug in half.

69. Once you've established a good relationship with a vet and he or she is familiar with your pet's health status, call for home care suggestions when minor problems arise instead of visiting the clinic. You may be able to avoid an office visit.

70. House solitary animals, such as hamsters and rabbits, separately to avoid fights and vet bills.

71. Pick up a big apron at a thrift store to wear when you groom pets.

72. Instead of buying a grooming table to groom small pets, place a rubber mat on top of the washer, dryer or kitchen counter.

73. Don't pay a portrait studio to photograph your pet. Take the photos yourself, then request extra prints.

74. Trim rabbit, cat, bird, guinea pig and (small) puppy toenails with ordinary human nail trimmers. Not only will you avoid the expense of purchasing special trimmers, but they work great.

75. Save old bedspreads, blankets and sheets. Place in crates to make a comfy den.

76. Don't buy a special pet gate to keep pets out of certain areas of the house. Baby gates are less expensive and an easy yard-sale find.

77. Buy canned food by the case, instead of one can at a time.

78. Store grooming supplies in a large cosmetic case or small tool box.

79. Buy large bottles of generic aspirin for arthritic pets (with your veterinarian's approval, of course).

80. If you're handy at tying knots, make a bird toy from cotton rope, bells and rawhide, or macramé a pet collar.

81. Build an aviary.

82. To prevent hair balls, be sure to give rabbits plenty of hay and exercise during heavy molting.

83. Clean droppings from the sides of bird cages by simply soaking in hot water. Don't use bleach; it can cause cages to rust.

84. If you don't have a computer and Internet access, check with the public library. Many libraries have online services.

85. Give bunny a treat right from the yard: dandelions, pansies, curly kale and parsley. Make sure no pesticides have been sprayed, though.

86. Line the bird's travel cage or case with felt, and eliminate perches. This gives the bird something soft to hang onto while driving and lessens the chance it might lose its balance on a perch.

87. Locate custom terrarium cage plans on the Internet.

88. Veterinary schools are an excellent resource, especially for pets with unusual or difficult problems. If there's a school nearby, find out if there's a clinic.

89. Make an Elizabethan collar with sturdy cardboard and heavy-duty tape to keep a pet from licking wounds or pulling out stitches.

90. Don't buy an "ant proof" pet bowl, make one. Place the pet's dish within a larger dish or pan filled with water. The moat discourages all but the most adventurous ants.

91. Use a towel as a sling to support a pet with weak hindquarters.

92. Make a flea trap. Place a sheet of white paper on the floor and put a pie pan filled with water on the paper. Add a little dishwashing detergent. At night, place a reading lamp over the pan. Check for overnight guests in the morning.

93. Use baking soda to clean up pet messes. It will soak up moisture and eliminate odor. Be sure to use generously. Club soda works well to eliminate odors, too.

94. Pick up a used fish tank (good condition, no cracks) at a thrift store or garage sale to house reptiles and amphibians, or small mammals.

95. Cardboard egg cartons are great hiding places for very small mammals.

96. Save margarine tubs. Use as traveling containers for amphibians. Cover with nylon mesh.

97. Use a plastic baby bathtub to bathe small pets. They're easily found, and inexpensive, at thrift shops.

98. Make a muzzle from a long strip of fairly wide gauze.

99. Use your hair dryer to dry a pet after bathing.

100. Last, but not least, ask for a discount. Many store owners will give a 10 to 20 percent discount if you pay cash, but you won't know that if you don't ask.

CHAPTER 10

Resources: When You Need Help

A budget tells us what we can't afford, but it doesn't keep us from buying it.
—William Feather

Need help? We all have times in our lives when we need a helping hand. Pet owners are no exception. Although there is no formal national organization to assist owners in the midst of a crisis (there should be!), financial or otherwise, there are thousands of organizations, large and small, and even more individual animal lovers who can help in a variety of ways.

Some organizations provide free information; a care booklet on rabbits and cavies, for example. Others offer advice for a dog's behavior problem or counsel on which animal species might be appropriate for a family. Veterinarians volunteer their skills for low-cost spay/neuter clinics; a neighbor pays for a ferret's vaccinations. Dedicated animal lovers wish the best for every pet and will go to great lengths to help struggling owners.

Perhaps you need assistance. Could, or would, someone help you? Absolutely. But there's a catch.

Remember, reducing your pet-care budget requires effort. You must learn to budget, practice preventive care and be a smart shopper. The same effort is required for assistance in the midst of trouble. You will probably have to search for it, and it may take several telephone calls before you find the right help.

Even though resources are plentiful, don't expect a bucket of cash. It won't happen, unless, of course, you win the lottery. More likely, you'll find a free or very low cost vaccination or spay/neuter clinic; a free bag or case of pet food; free boarding for animals belonging to domestic violence victims; an information packet or book on the animal species you're thinking about adopting; the telephone number of an organization that can help you; manufacturers' coupons; encouragement and advice on how to keep a pet in spite of its annoying behavior problems or samples of a new grooming product.

Here's a brief listing of national resources that will give you a head start on seeking help. Following that, take a look at your local Yellow Pages (see listings under "Animals," "Animal Shelters," "Humane Societies" and "Pets") for organizations in your area. Check out the local library and what's online, too. Most organizations have Internet sites. Remember, there are animal lovers who don't even know you who care about you and your pet. If you need help, don't delay. Call, write or send an e-mail message today!

Humane Organizations

American Humane Association
63 Inverness Dr. East
Englewood, CO 80112
(800) 227-4645

National animal protection organization. A free membership magazine is available upon request, as well as referrals to organizations in your area.

The Humane Society of the United States
2100 L St., NW
Washington, DC 20037
(202) 452-1100

National animal protection organization. Does not operate local humane societies. Free brochures, with SASE, on responsible pet care, etc., for individuals; provides some local referrals.

Animal Clubs and Organizations

SPAY/USA
750 Port Washington Blvd.
Ste. 2
Port Washington, NY 11050
(800) 248-SPAY

National referral service for low-cost spay/neuter clinics. Approximately 6,000 participating veterinarians. There is no charge for referral; pay the local vet directly. Spay/neuter educational materials are for sale.

Friends of Animals
Low-Cost Spay/Neuter Clinic
P.O. Box 30054
Hartford, CT 06150-0054
(800) 321-PETS

National referral program of Friends of Animals. There is no charge for referral; pay FOA to receive a spay/neuter certificate for a local, partici-pating vet.

American Veterinary Medical Association
1931 N. Meacham Rd.
Ste. 100
Schaumburg, IL 60173-4360
(800) 248-2862

Dedicated to advancing the science and art of veterinary medicine. Encourages owners to discuss pet-care needs with a veterinarian. Free educational brochures (single copy) on topics such as vaccines, traveling with pets or diseases are available on request.

American Holistic Veterinary Medical Association
2214 Old Emmorton Rd.
Bel Air, MD 21015
(410) 569-0795

Dedicated to encouraging the alternative approaches to veterinary medi-cine. Send a SASE for a list of holistic veterinarians in your area.

American Kennel Club

5580 Centerview Dr.
Raleigh, NC 27606-3390
(919) 233-9767
http://www.akc.org

Purebred dog registry. Call with specific requests.

Cat Fanciers Association

1805 Atlantic Ave.
P.O. Box 1005
Manasquan, NJ 08736-0805
(908) 528-9797
http://www.cfainc.org

Purebred cat registry. Call with specific requests.

Delta Society

289 Perimeter Rd. East
Renton, WA 98055-1329
(800) 869-6898
TDD (800) 809-2714

Dedicated to exploring the bond between animals and people. Delta Society provides information (some free, most for sale) on seniors and pets, service dogs, pet therapy, pet loss, AIDS and pets, housing and pets or therapeutic horseback riding. Call with specific requests.

American Grooming Shop Association

4575 Galley Rd.
Ste. 400A
Colorado Springs, CO 80915
(719) 570-7788
E-mail: groomshop@aol.com
http://www.abka.com/agsa.htm

Professional trade association for grooming shop owners and operators. Call or write for free listing of AGSA members.

American Boarding Kennels Association

4575 Galley Rd.
Ste. 400A
Colorado Springs, CO 80915
(719) 591-1113
E-mail: petsabka@aol.com
http://www.abka.com

*Professional trade association for boarding kennel owners and operators.
Call or write for a free listing of ABKA members.*

American Federation of Aviculture

P.O. Box 56218
Phoenix, AZ 85079-6218
(602) 484-0931

*Member organization dedicated to bird conservation, captive breeding
and education. Call with requests.*

American Federation of Herpetoculturists

P.O. Box 300067
Escondido, CA 92030
(619) 561-4948

*Educates the public and legislative representatives about reptiles and
amphibians. Call or write with requests.*

Rat, Mouse and Hamster Fanciers

C/o Joyce Starkey
2309 Country Ranch Dr.
Modesto, CA 95355
E-mail: 102641.3365@compuserve.com

*Breed fancier club dedicated to sharing knowledge about rats, mice and
hamsters, improving breeds and having fun. Membership is $15 yearly.
Information and referrals are available; brochures for sale.*

American Rabbit Breeders Association, Inc.

P.O. Box 426
Bloomington, IL 61702
(309) 664-7500
E-mail: arbamail@aol.com
http://www.members@aol.com/arbanet/arba/web

Member organization dedicated to providing proper information on raising and exhibiting rabbits and cavies. Free brochures on rabbit and cavy care, breeding, feeding and showing are available upon request, as well as referrals to local clubs (2,000 nationwide). Yearly dues are $15.

House Rabbit Society

P.O. Box 1201
Alameda, CA 94501
(510) 521-4631

Member organization dedicated to rescuing and caring for rabbits. They provide rabbit care brochures and seminars. Yearly dues are $12.

Shelters That Adopt and Rescue Ferrets (STAR)

P.O. Box 1714
Springfield, VA 22151-0714
(703) 354-5073

Network of individuals and organizations that work with ferrets. They provide education, and aid adoption and rescue.

F.A.I.R. (Ferret Adoption, Information and Rescue)

P.O. Box 952
Westmont, IL 60559
(630) 968-3189

Dedicated to educating the public about ferrets and their care. They provide information, and aid adoption and rescue.

Hot Lines

Animal Behavior Helpline
Sponsored by the San Francisco Society
for the Prevention of Cruelty to Animals
(415) 554-3075

Offers behavior information for dogs and cats. Consultation is free, except for applicable long-distance charges. Charges reversed for return calls.

Consumer Credit Counseling Services
(800) 388-CCCS (2227)

Offers referrals to a nonprofit credit counselor. Has 700 offices in the United States. Consultations are free.

Federal Trade Commission
(202)326-2222

Call for a list of free FTC publications aimed at protecting consumers, including brochures and booklets giving advice on credit, investment scams or shopping.

Friskies Pet Care
(800) 366-6033

Offers pet nutrition and product information. Written materials on topics such as obesity, pet loss and training are available upon request. Consultation and calls are free.

Hill's Pet Nutrition Line
(800) 445-5777

Offers pet nutrition and product information. Written materials, including feeding guidelines, training and disease information are available upon request. Consultation and calls are free.

Iams Pet Nutrition Hotline
(800) 525-4267

Offers pet nutrition and care information, as well as product information. Written materials are available upon request. Consultation and calls are free.

Purina
(800) 776-7526

Offers pet nutrition and product information. Written materials available upon request. Consultation and calls are free.

Pet Loss Support Helpline
Sponsored by the Chicago Veterinary Medical Association
(630) 603-3994

Offers pet loss support counseling. Consultation and calls are free, except for applicable long-distance charges.

Pet Loss Support Hotline
Sponsored by the University of California
at Davis School of Veterinary Medicine
(916) 752-4200

Offers pet loss support counseling. Materials are available upon request. Consultation is free except for applicable long-distance charges; charges reversed on return call.

Poison Control Center
Sponsored by the National Animal Poison
Control Center at the University of Illinois
(800) 548-2423 or (900) 680-0000

Offers poison control information from veterinarians. The 800 number is for veterinarians and pet owners, and costs $30 per case; major credit cards accepted. The 900 number is for nonemergency questions and costs $20 for the first five minutes, then $2.95 a minute, with a $20 minimum.

Tree House Hotline
Sponsored by Tree House Animal Foundation
(773) 784-5488
TDD (773) 784-5605

Offers information and advice on dogs and cats. Consultation is free, except for applicable long-distance charges.

Books

Cat Owner's Home Veterinary Handbook. Delbert G. Carlson, D.V.M. and James M. Giffin, M.D., Howell Book House, 1992.

Consumer's Resource Handbook. United States Office of Consumer Affairs (Consumer Information Center, Pueblo, CO 81009).

Dog Owner's Home Veterinary Handbook. Delbert G. Carlson, D.V.M. and James M. Giffin, M.D., Howell Book House, 1992.

Dr. Pitcairn's Complete Guide to Natural Health for Dogs and Cats. Richard H. Pitcairn, D.V.M., Ph.D., and Susan Hubble Pitcairn, Rodale Press, 1995.

How to Pinch a Penny Till It Screams. Rochelle LaMotte McDonald, Avery Publishing Group, 1994.

How to Save Money on Just About Everything. William Roberts, Strebor Publications, 1991.

If Time Is Money, No Wonder I'm Not Rich. Mary L. Sprouse, Simon & Schuster, 1993.

The Illustrated Veterinary Guide for Dogs, Cats, Birds and Exotic Pets. Chris Pinney, D.V.M., McGraw-Hill, 1992.

Kiplinger's Facing 40. Daniel Moreau, Kiplinger Books, 1993.

The Money Book of Personal Finance. Richard Eisenberg, Warner Books, 1996.

Money Talks. Bob Rosefsky, McGraw-Hill, 1989.

The Penny Pincher's Almanac. Dean King and the editors of *The Penny Pincher's Almanac,* Fireside Books, 1992.

Shopping Smart. John Stossell, G.P. Putnam's Sons, 1980.

Straight Talk on Money. Ken and Daria Dolan, Simon & Schuster, 1993.

The Super Saver. Janet Lowe, Longman Financial Services Publishing, 1990.

The Tightwad Gazette. Amy Dacyczyn, Villard Books, 1993.

Two Incomes and Still Broke? Linda Kelley, Times Books, 1996.

The Way to Save. Ginita Wall, Henry Holt, 1994.

About the Author

Virginia Parker Guidry is a long-time animal enthusiast, writer and editor on a budget. Ms. Guidry graduated from Berea College in Berea, Kentucky, with a BA in English. Her editorial experience includes staff positions with newspapers and magazines, including *Dog Fancy* and *Horse Illustrated*. Ms. Guidry has also worked as a professional small animal groomer, horse groom and veterinary assistant. When she is not writing or editing, she can be found searching for bargains and planning ways to fund her pet habit on a freelancer's budget.

Index